American Illustration 10

American Illustration 10

Edited by Edward Booth-Clibborn

celebrating the tenth annual of American editorial, advertising, poster, book, promotion art, maps and charts, unpublished work, and film animation.

Watson-Guptill Publications   New York

Editor: Edward Booth-Clibborn
Project Director: Bonnie Claeys Smith
Designer: Michael Mabry
Assistant Designers: Keiko Hayashi, Sandy Lee

The artwork and the caption information in this book have been supplied by the entrants. While every effort has been made to ensure accuracy, American Illustration, Inc. does not under any circumstances accept any responsibility for errors or omissions.

If you are a practicing illustrator, artist, or student, and would like to submit work to the next annual competition, write to:
American Illustration, Inc.
49 East 21st Street
New York, NY 10010
(212) 979-4500.

Distributor to the U.S.A. Trade:
Watson-Guptill Publications
1515 Broadway
New York, NY 10036 U.S.A.
ISBN 8230-6068-3

Distributed in the United Kingdom and World Direct Mail:
Internos Books
18 Colville Road
London W3 8BL U.K.

Distributor in France
Sofedis
29 Rue Saint-Sulpice
Paris 75006
France

Book trade for the rest of the world:
Hearst Books International
105 Madison Avenue
New York, NY 10016 U.S.A.

Copyright © 1991
Call for Entries
American Illustration, Inc.
Printed and bound in Japan by Dai Nippon
All rights reserved.
No part of this publication may be reproduced, stored in a retrieval system, or transmitted in any form or by any means, electronic, mechanical, photocopying, recording, or otherwise, without prior permission of the copyright owners.

INTRODUCTION
Edward Booth-Clibborn
reflects about the past ten years
of American Illustration.
№ 6

JURY
Laurie Kelliher, Terry Koppel,
John Korpics, Diana LaGuardia,
Michael Mabry, Bob Manley,
Francoise Mouly, Frank Olinsky,
David Pickel, Rhonda Rubinstein
№ 8

EDITORIAL
Illustrations for newspapers
and their supplements,
and consumer, trade, and technical
magazines and periodicals.
№ 16

BOOKS
Cover and interior
illustrations for all types of
fiction and non-fiction books.
№ 78

ADVERTISING
Illustrations used in
advertising in consumer, trade, and
professional magazines.
№ 102

POSTERS
Poster illustrations for
consumer products, institutions,
and special events.
№ 108

PROMOTION
Illustrations for
brochures, record albums, and
self-promotional use.
№ 116

MAPS AND CHARTS
Maps and charts for magazines
and promotional use.
№ 138

UNPUBLISHED WORK
Commissioned but unpublished
illustrations, and personal work
produced by professionals
and students.
№ 144

FILM AND VIDEO
Illustrations used in
music videos, computer graphics,
feature films, documentaries, and
educational or promotional films.
№ 170

SPECIAL PROJECTS
Illustration that does not come
through the usual publishing channels,
such as, non-profit community
projects, magazines, etc.
№ 174

INTRODUCTION CONTINUES
Edward Booth-Clibborn's
reflections about the past ten years.
It includes a listing of all
illustrators who have ever been
published in this prestigious annual.
№ 180

INDEX:
Names and addresses of
contributing artists; names of
Art Directors, Designers,
Publications, Publishers, Design
Groups, Advertising Agencies,
Writers, and Clients etc. who were
involved in the creation and
use of these images.
№ 192

Introduction by Edward Booth-Clibborn

If a week is a long time in politics, ten years is an age in the life of an annual like "American Illustration." Or so some might say.

For me, it doesn't seem a decade too long.

I can still remember how, in Paris at the 1980 launch of what was then our seventh "European Illustration" annual exhibition, Sue Coe encouraged me to bring the same idea to America. It was, she said, badly needed. For her, the well established American Society of Illustrators was no longer representative of the people working in the USA. Its juries were far too political, and too often made up almost exclusively of illustrators. The books they produced seemed long ago to have given up trying to make the individual items look good.

Then, in April 1981, I had a call from Robert Priest. As Art Director of Esquire Magazine, he had been talking to other New York Art Directors, and to Sue Coe, and they all believed America was more than ready for an annual produced to the same high standards as "European Illustration." And one containing work selected under the same kind of rules.

How could I resist their enthusiasm? Or to reject their encouragement?

More importantly, how could we make it work?

The idea becomes reality

On June 8th 1981, the first meeting of the first "American Illustration" committee took place in Julian Allen's studio in New York. Those present with Julian and I were: Robert Priest (Art Director, Esquire Magazine), Nigel Holmes (Assistant Art Director, TIME Magazine), Mary Shanahan (Art Director, Rolling Stone), Marshall Arisman (Illustrator and Co-Chairperson of Media Arts at the New York School of Visual Arts), Linda Johnson (Art Director, TONIGHT), Steve Heller (Art Director, The New York Times Book Review) and Mark Crawford (Editor-in-Chief, Time Capsule Inc.).

From the outset, it was clear that the annual of the Society of Illustrators was suffering from all the shortcomings Sue Coe had outlined, and some more. Not only was it repetitive year after year, it was also late year after year.

I outlined the principles which have always underpinned our "European Illustration" series, and proposed that they be adopted for a new "American Illustration" annual.

Put briefly, these are:

that each year's jury should consist only of established art directors and art editors who commission illustrative work for the media;

that the jury should devote itself to the pursuit of excellence, committing itself to selecting only work which is both well conceived and well executed;

that the annual should be divided into two main sections (commissioned and published work for print and film media, and unpublished work in any medium) and open to professionals and students alike;

that the annual would feature one illustration per page;

and that there would be no awards, on that grounds that having work selected for publication would be an award in itself.

Ten years on, we are still abiding by those same principles.

And ten years on, the effects of the introduction of "American Illustration" can easily be seen.

A route to recognition

Many illustrators such as Matt Mahurin, Vivienne Fletcher and others had their early work accepted by our first juries. As the years have gone by, we've seen their talents and techniques develop, and they've become well established names with work in our annual year after year.

Of course, some years have seen better work than others (though we've never had a truly bad year). What matters is that our overall standards have ensured that this annual has become the benchmark of excellence for all American illustrators.

But "American Illustration" has always been much more than just an annual.

From the beginning, we wanted to create a forum for the development of illustration right across the American continent. And we wanted to find a way of defining the true characteristics of North American illustration.

As you'll see from my very personal selection of images from

continued on page 180

American Illustration 10 Jury

Laurie Kelliher: Little is known about her early life. ~~years~~ For the past two years Laurie has served as Senior designer at MTV networks, where she has created award-winning PRINT material for MTV, Nickelodean, and Nick at nite.

№ 8

Terry Koppel: A former Art Director of the Boston Globe, Terry went on to found Koppel & Scher with Paula Scher. Projects have included designs for ART & Antiques, V magazine, and the original design for European Travel & Life. He is currently Art Director of RedBook, and has recieved awards from the N.Y. Art Directors Club, Graphis, and AIGA among others. His work is in the collections of the Library of Congress, MOMA, and the Georges Pompidou Museum in Paris. № 9

John Korpics: after graduating from Carnegie-Mellon university, JOHN worked freelance before joining Philadelphia Magazine as designer. In January 1988 he moved to REGARDIE'S magazine, and took over as ART DIRECTOR in May of that year. John's WORK has appeared in American Photography, American illustration, SPD Design annual, and Communication ARts photography and Illustration annuals.

Diana LaGuardia: Beginnig her career at a small news paper in MAINE, Diana went on to design Francis Ford Coppola's magazine, CITY of San Francisco. She was Art Director at the New York Times magazine for two years, after which she joined Conde Nast in 1988. Currently Art Director at Conde Nast Traveler, Diana has recieved numerous awards in publication and Book design, and served as President of the Society of Publication Designers for three years.

Michael Mabry: Prior to starting his own firm, Michael Mabry Design Inc., Michael worked for Sidjakov, Berman and Gomez as senior designer and University of Utah graphic design Group. He has recieved awards from Communications Arts, AIGA, Graphis, and others, and his work is among the permanent collections of the Library of congress and included in an exhibition on California Design at Museo Fortuny in Venice.

№ 11

Bob Manley:

 Bob is partner and Creative Director of Altman and Manley/Eagle Advertising, a small advertising and design studio in Manchester, New Hampshire. The company's work has been featured in a number of graphic design publications, including Graphis, Communication Arts, and Print Magazine, and has won awards in the Art Directors Club of NY, AIGA and CLIO Awards. In recent years, Bob has become an accomplished driver in snowy conditions.

Francoise Mouly:

Francoise has been the co-editor and Art director of RAW magazine since its inception ten years ago. RAW is currently published by Penguin Books, and Francoise remains active in the graphic design community.

Frank Olinsky: A partner in Manhattan Design, Frank has worked on album packages for 10,000 Maniacs, R.E.M., the B-52's, and others. He worked on the original look and chameleon-like logo for MTV: Music Television, and is co-author with David Byrne of "What the Songs Look Like — contemporary Artists Interpret Talking Heads Songs." Other projects have included posters, books, and film and video animation.

№ 13

David Pickel: currently Design Director of the Plain Dealer Sunday magazine. David's past postions have included Features page Designer at the PLAIN DEALER and Picture Editor at the Louisville COURIER-Journal. He holds a MASTER of Science degree in journalism, and has recieved honors from the National Press photographers Association, the Houston ART Directors Club and the Cleveland museum of ART.

Rhonda Rubinstein! after working her way though the Newstand, Rhonda has stopped periodically at Newsweek, GQ, Smart, and her current position as ART DIRECTOR of Esquire. Her work has been recognized in numerous typography and publication design annuals, and was recently featured in the Canadian exhibition "NOW from NEW YORK". an un-designer-like affinities for words has landed Rhonda's articles in publications such as Creative Review and The Manipulator, and she has Lectured at FOLIO, McLean Hunter Publishing Seminar, and NYU'S School of Journalism.

№ 15

Editorial: trade and ALL types including technical drawings. →

Consumer, tehnical Magazines, of illustrations, CARTOONS, comic strips, Architectural Newspapers and their supplements.

Philippe Lardy

Publication: Newsday Magazine, December 1990   Publishing Company: Times-Mirror

Oil on canvas   № 19

Art Director: Jackie Segal   Writer: Stanley Green
Publication: Newsday Magazine, December 1990   Publishing Company: Times-Mirror
This piece, entitled "A Surreal View of the Sexes" was presented in an article about the artist.
Oil on canvas   № 19

Blair Drawson

Art Director: Carmen Dunjko   Designer: Scott Gibbs
Publication: Saturday Night Magazine, December 1990   Publishing Company: Saturday Night Magazine Inc.
"Tree of Knowledge" served as the cover for Wildwood, a literary supplement to Saturday Night Magazine.
Acrylic

№ 20

Ross MacDonald

Art Director: Carmen Dunjko   Designer: Jill Dickie
Publication: Saturday Night Magazine, April 1990   Publishing Company: Saturday Night Magazine Inc.
The concept of refugee dreams inspired this cover illustration for the Wildwood literary supplement.
Watercolor
№ 21

Tony Fitzpatrick

Art Director: Tom Staebler   Designer: Kristen Korjenek
Publication: Playboy Magazine, October 1990   Publishing Company: Playboy
Poet/writer/artist Fitzpatrick created this image to accompany his article on the
Tyson-Douglas fight entitled, "In This Corner."
Pastel and pencil   № 22

Janet Woolley

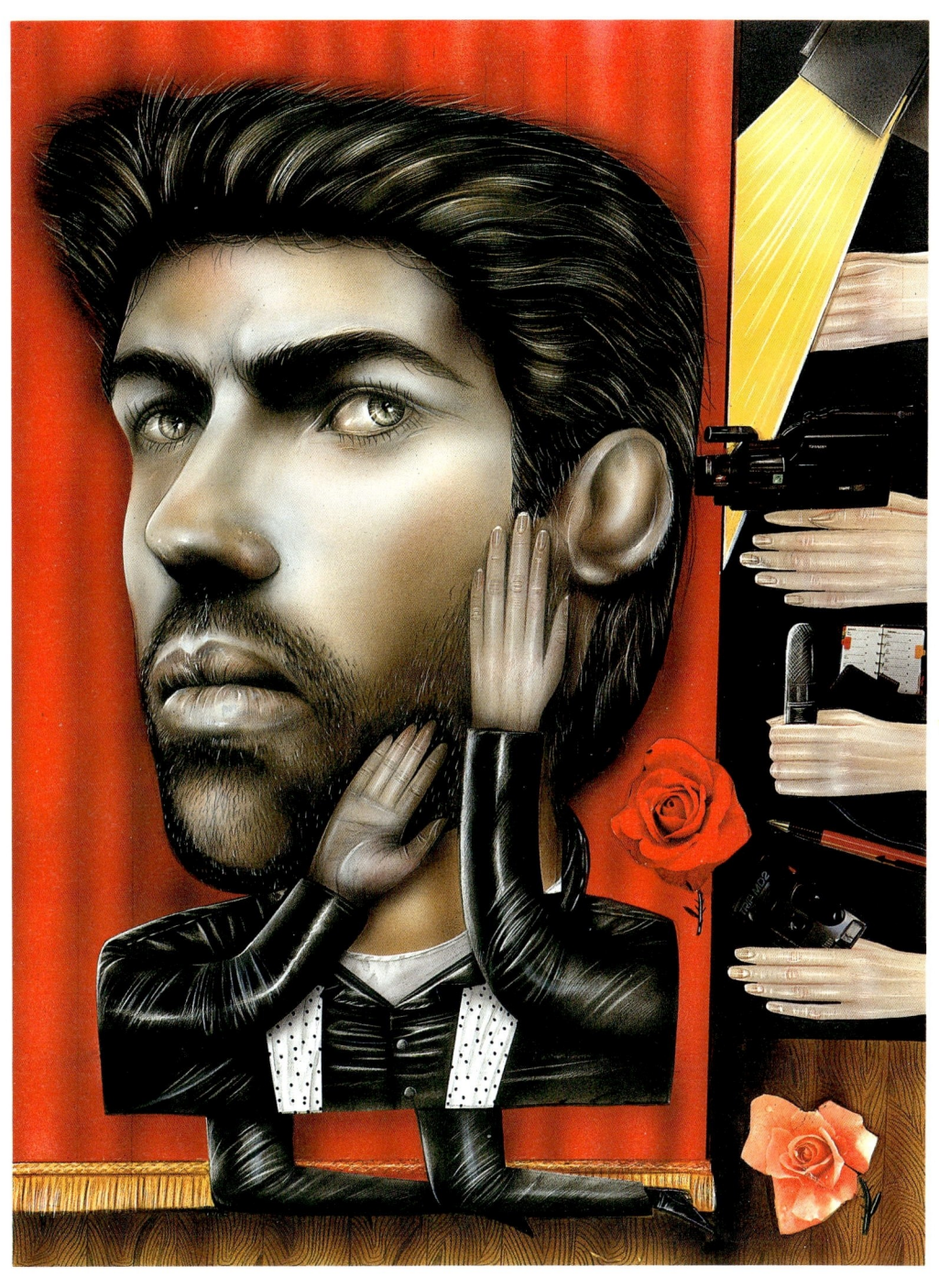

Art Director: Jolene Cuyler Designer: Mark Shafer Writer: Bob Hofler
Publication: US Magazine, December 1990 Publishing Company: Straight Arrow Publishers
Another image in "Star '90," this time showing George Michael and his expressed displeasure with star status.
Acrylic, pencil, and collage

Janet Woolley

Art Director: Nancy Smith
Publication: Ms. Magazine, September 1990   Publishing Company: Lang Communications
This image appeared on the cover of a special report issue entitled "Everyday Violence Against Women."
Acrylic and collage   № 24

Janet Woolley

Art Director: Doug Renfro   Designer: Andrea Burns   Writer: Jack Hitt
Publication: Special Report, 1990   Publishing Company: Whittle Communications
"Pay the Cashier, Your Lordship," an article on buying titles in Great Britain, featured this illustration.
Oil and mixed medium collage   № 25

Philip Burke

Design Director: Michael Grossman   Designer: Robert Newman   Writer: Giselle Benatar
Publication: Entertainment Weekly, October 1990   Publishing Company: Time-Warner Inc.
The article "Doctor Doom" featured this image of Kurt Vonnegut.
Oil on canvas   № 26

Philip Burke

Design Director: Michael Grossman   Designer: Mark Michaelson
Publication: Entertainment Weekly, May 1990   Publishing Company: Time-Warner Inc.
The article "Why are we still watching Thirtysomething?" included this image of adman Miles Drenttel.
Oil on canvas   № 27

Philip Burke

Publication: Mother Jones Magazine, March 1991

Art Director: Kerry Tremain   Designer: Marsha Sessa   Writer: Stephen Talbot
Publication: Mother Jones Magazine, March 1991   Publishing Company: Foundation for National Progress
Film director Oliver Stone was the subject of this portrait for the article "60's Something."
oil on canvas   № 28

Philip Burke

№29

Art Director: Jolene Cuyler   Designer: Mark Shafer   Writer: Bob Hofler
Publication: US Magazine, December 1990   Publishing Company: Straight Arrow Publishers
Actress Julia Roberts as a character in Picasso's "Les Demoiselles D'avignon" appeared in the article "Star '90."
Oil on canvas

Mick Aarestrup

Art Director: Kevin Hein
Publication: Havoc, July 1990   Publishing Company: Rayocine Studios
The effects of apartment living are portrayed in the comic strip, "Neighbors."
Linoleum cut

John Kleber

Art Director: Sara Christensen   Designer: Julie Belcher   Writer: Cathy Schecter
Publication: Special Reports/Health, February 1991   Publishing Company: Whittle Communications
Seasonal Affective Disorder and the effects of Light Therapy inspired this image, which accompanied the article
"A New Light on Winter Blues."
Monoprint

Scott Menchin

№32

Art Director: Lucy Bartholomay   Writer: Norman Boucher
Publication: The Boston Globe Magazine, September 1990   Publishing Company: Affiliated Publications, Inc.
This illustration captured the writer's emotional journey as he faced his father's illness in "My Father's Heart."
Pen and ink   №32

Brad Holland

№ 33

Art Director: Richard Bleiweiss   Writer: Steven A. Emerson
Publication: Penthouse Magazine, March 1991   Publishing Company: Penthouse
This image appeared with the article "Journey Into Fear," about a high-ranking Arab terrorist who defected to the U.S.
Acrylic on masonite

Brad Holland

Art Director: D.J. Stout   Designer: Nancy McMillen   Writer: Robert Bryce
Publication: Texas Monthly, February 1991   Publishing Company: Texas Monthly Magazine
The shortage of potable water in Texas is the subject of "More Precious Than Oil"
Acrylic on masonite №34

Brad Holland

Art Director: Hans-Georg Pospischil   Writer: Von Ingrid Heinrich-Jost
Publication: Frankfurter Allgemeine Magazin, December 1990   Publishing Company: Frankfurter All. Zeitung
Featured in the article "Unter dem Pflaster," this image is one in a series concerning life in the subways.
Acrylic on masonite   №35

Stefano Vitale

Art Director: Pamela Berry   Writer: Amanda Spake
Publication: Savvy Woman, April 1990   Publishing Company: Family Media
An article on caring for elderly parents inspired these two illustrations.
Oil on canvas

Stefano Vitale

Henrik Drescher

Art Director: Jane Palecek   Writer: Lisa Davis
Publication: In Health Magazine, March 1990   Publishing Company: Hippocrates, Inc.
"Grounded," an article on the fear of flying, included this illustration of a man caged.
Mixed media   №38

Gary Baseman

Art Director: Sara Christensen   Designer: Julie Belcher   Writer: Laura Fissinger
Publication: Special Report/Family, November 1990   Publishing Company: Whittle Communications
Acrylic

In an article on sexual ethics, this series explores:
Unfaithfulness,   № 39

Gary Baseman

The AIDS epidemic,
№ 40

Gary Baseman

Co-habitation and family reactions.

J. Otto Seibold

Art Director: Judy Garlan   Designer: Robin Gilmore-Barnes   Writer: Lee Clarke
Publication: The Atlantic Monthly, November 1990   Publishing Company: The Atlantic Monthly Corp.
The article "Oil-Spill Fantasies" gave rise to a series of illustrations depicting the handling of the
Great Alaskan Oil Spill crisis.
Adobe Illustrator   № 42

J. Otto Seibold

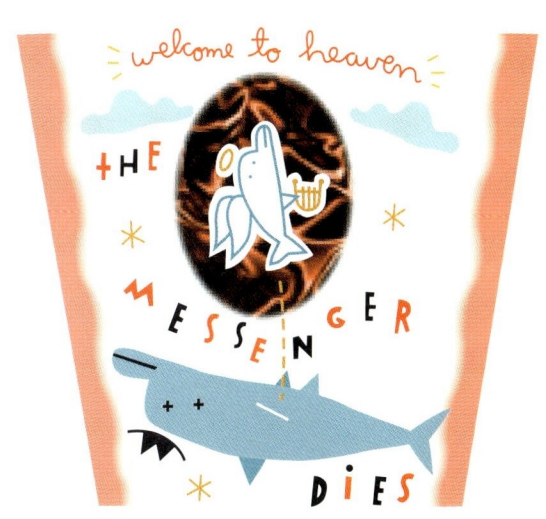

№ 43

J. Otto Seibold

Frank Viva

Art Director: Nancy V. Kent Writers: Miriam Shuchman, Michael Wilkes
Publication: Good Health Magazine, October 1990 Publishing Company: The New York Times
Drug therapy versus psychotherapy is the subject of "Dramatic Progress Against Depression."
Chalk and watercolor № 46

steven Guarnaccia

Art Director: David Pickel   Writer: Dana Kennedy
Publication: Plain Dealer Magazine   Publishing Company: The Plain Dealer Publishing Co.
"In Bean We Trust" explored the pervasive influence of L.L. Bean clothing on American fashion.
This illustration appeared on the cover.
Marker, colored pencils on brown paper   № 47

Steven Guarnaccia

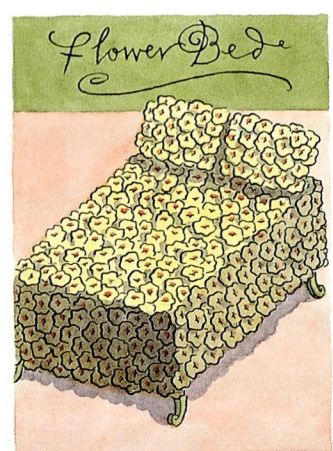

Art Director: Don Morris
Publication: Metropolitan Home, 1990   Publishing Company: Meredith Corporation
The illustration series "Home Truths" looks at homes, furnishings, and how people really live.
Pen and ink, watercolor № 48

Steven Guarnaccia

Philippe Weisbecker

Art Director: Paul Davis   Designer: Risa Zaitschek
Publication: WigWag, 1990   Publishing Company: WigWag Magazine Company
One in a series of ten drawings created for use as magazine section dividers.
Pencil and watercolor

David Ricceri

Art Director: Neill McCutcheon   Designer: Jill Andrews   Writer: Georgia Routsis
Publication: Sassy Magazine, January 1990   Publishing Company: Sassy Publishers, Inc.
"Capricorn, the Goat" is one in a series of twelve signs of the zodiac created
for use in the monthly "Signs" column.
Pen and ink   №51

Anita Kunz

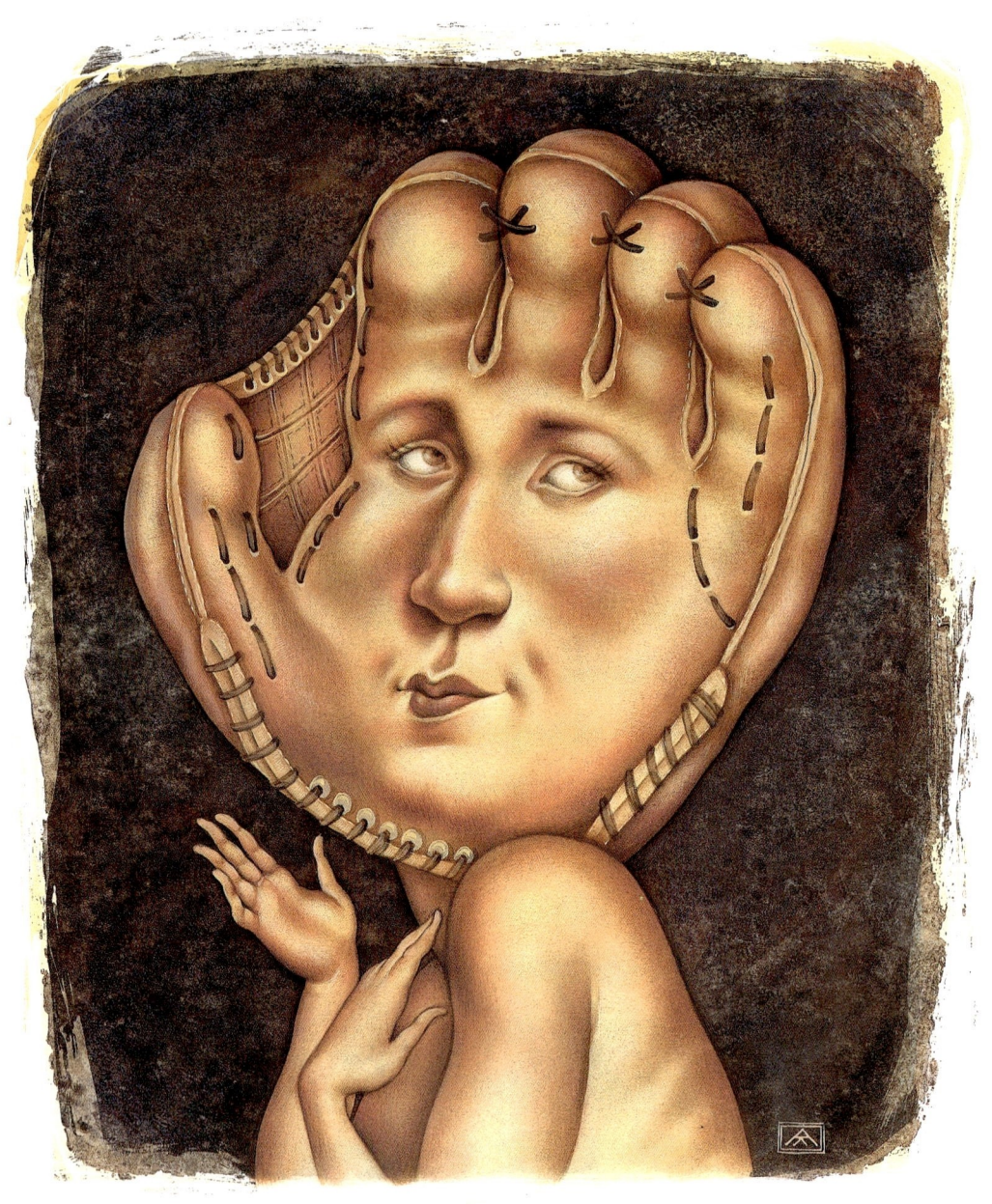

Art Director: Steven Hoffman   Designer: Teresa Fernandez   Writers: Steve Wulf, Jim Kaplan
Publication: Sports Illustrated, May 1990   Publishing Company: Time-Warner Inc.
"Glove Story" explores the baseball glove as an American icon.
This image portrays the practice of naming a mitt after a woman.
Watercolor and gouache   № 52

Malcolm Tarlofsky

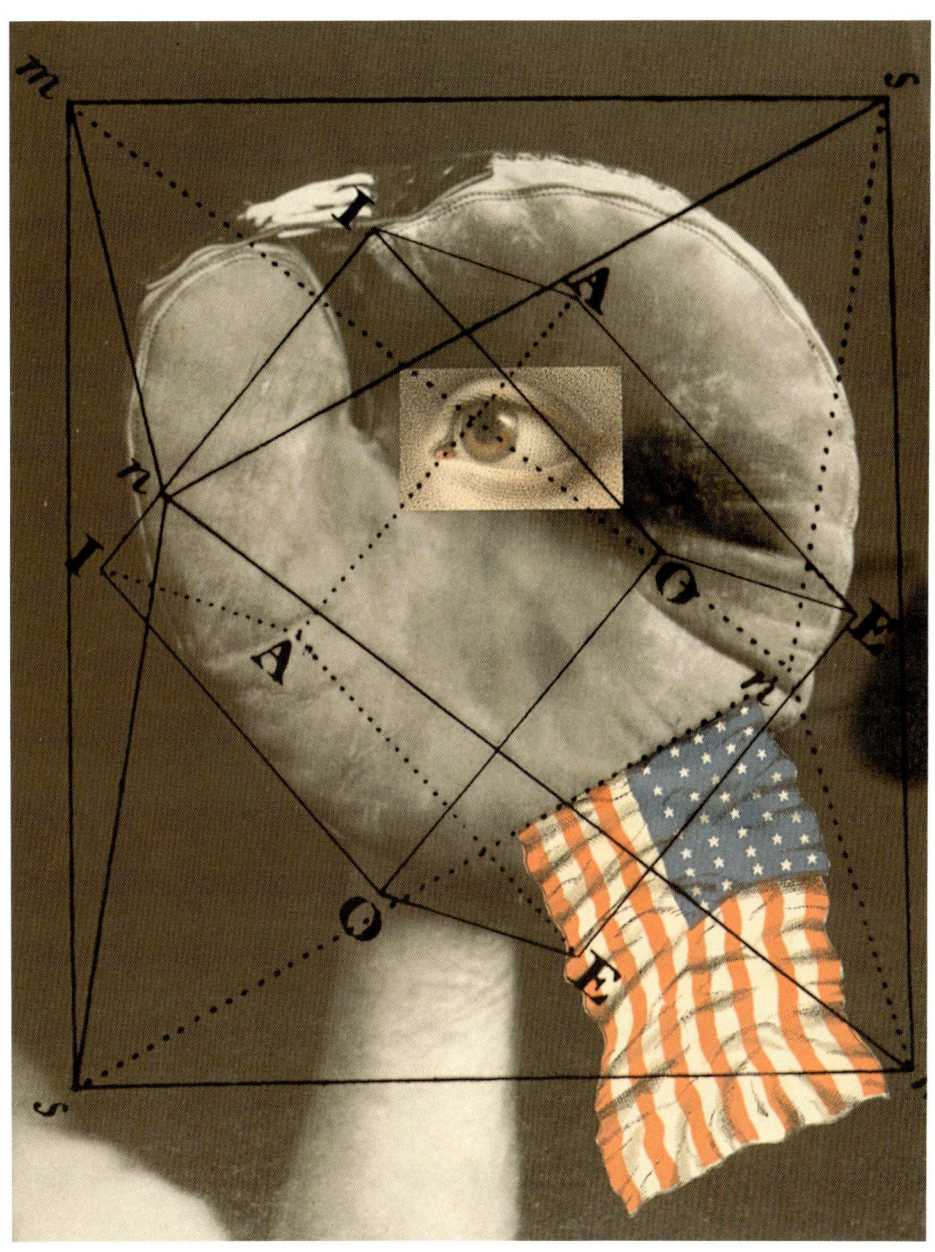

Art Director: Steven Hoffman   Designer: Teresa Fernandez   Writer: Steve Wulf, Jim Kaplan
Publication: Sports Illustrated, May 1990   Publishing Company: Time-Warner Inc.
Also from "Glove Story," an illustration focusing on the catcher's glove and its geometric properties.

Brian Cronin

Art Director: F. Wilson
Publication: Longevity Magazine, January 1991   Publishing Company: General Media
This image accompanied an article on altering genes so they will reject Alzheimer's Disease.
Pen and ink, watercolor   № 54

Brian Cronin

Art Director: George Rambaldi
Publication: Lui Magazine, March 1991   Publishing Company: Lui Magazine
From "War in the Gulf," an article about the conflict in the Persian Gulf.
Pen and ink, watercolor
№55

Brian Cronin

Art Director: Fred Woodward   Designer: Gail Anderson   Writer: Robert L. Borosage
Publication: Rolling Stone, February 1991   Publishing Company: Straight Arrow Publishers
The article entitled, "How Bush Kept The Guns From Turning To Butter" featured these two illustrations.
Watercolor and colored pencil

Brian Cronin

Mick Wiggins

№ 58

Art Director: Joanne Hoffman   Writers: Doug Houseman, Anna O'Connell
Publication: Mac World Magazine   Fall 1990   Publishing Company: Mac World Communications
"Introduction to Modeling," an article on Computer Aided Design (CAD) environments, included this image.
Computer, digitized photo scraps   № 58

Joe Fleming

Art Director: Georges Haroutuin
Publication: Homemakers Magazine, Summer 1991   Publishing Company: Telemedia
Japanese and Californian philosophies on stress relief oppose each other in "East Meets West."
Acrylic on cut steel   № 59

Sue Coe

Design Director: Michael Grossman Designer: Anna Kula Writer: Ty Burr
Publication: Entertainment Weekly, February 1991 Publishing Company: Time-Warner Inc.
This illustration accompanied a review of consumer videotapes available on
Saddam Hussein and Operation Desert Shield.
Mixed Media
N° 60

Amy Guip

Art Director: Lisa Altomore   Design Director: Cathy Caldwell   Writer: Erica Abeel
Publication: New Woman Magazine   Publishing Company: Murdoch Magazines
Choosing between Women's Liberation and the happy homemaker, "The Straddle Generation" speaks of women who are torn between the two.
Mixed media   № 61

Seymour Chwast

Art Director: Hans-Georg Pospischil   Writer: Von Christopher Schwartz
Publication: Frankfurter Allgemeine Magazin, January 1990   Publishing Company: Frankfurter All. Zeitung
The series "My Home is My Castle" included this look at an imaginary home on the magazine cover.
Acrylic   № 62

Jose Ortega

Art Director: Paul Davis
Publication: Wigwag, February 1990   Publishing Company: Wigwag Magazine Company
This illustration of a car on a snowy road was the cover of Wigwag's winter issue.
Scratchboard and pastel   № 63

Laurie Rosenwald

Art Director: Douglas Riccardi   Designer: Laurie Rosenwald
Publication: Egg Magazine, August 1990   Publishing Company: Forbes
Created as a parody of Japanese magazines, this cover illustration highlights the features included in the issue.
Technical pen and templates

Douglas Fraser

Art Director: Nancy Harris   Writer: Lesley Hazleton
Publication: New York Times Magazine, October 1990   Publishing Company: The New York Times
The "Hers Column" featured this illustration in an article recounting the experience of a female journalist who worked as an auto mechanic for a week.

Jack Unruh

Art Director: Fred Woodward   Writer: David Frick
Publication: Rolling Stone, January 1990   Publishing Company: Straight Arrow Publishers
Bluesman Muddy Waters was the subject of this portrait which appeared with an album review.
Ink and watercolor   № 66

Lane Smith

Art Director: Fred Woodward   Writer: Paul Evens
Publication: Rolling Stone, November 1990   Publishing Company: Straight Arrow Publishers
Created to accompany a review of the INXS album "X", this image incorporates the song titles "Suicide Blonde,"
"Bitter Tears," and "Hear That Sound."
Oil on illustration board № 67

Lane Smith

Art Director: Fred Woodward   Writer: James Fallows
Publication: Rolling Stone, October 1990   Publishing Company: Straight Arrow Publishers
"The Best Years of Their Lives," an article about the Japanese college experience, included this illustration.
Oil on illustration board

Lane Smith

Art Director: David Carson   Writer: Nathan Newton
Publication: Beach Culture, May 1990   Publishing Company: Better Living Inc.
Pollution and toxic waste are the topics of "Is the End of Nature the Ultimate Fashion Statement?"
Oil on illustration board

Peter Kuper

№ 70

Art Director: Julie Simmons-Lynch   Designer: John Figurski
Publication: Heavy Metal, January 1991   Publishing Company: HM Communications
"Popeye" was included in the "Gallery" section of Heavy Metal, a visual feature spotlighting
the work of a different illustrator in each issue.
Stencil, enamel paint, colored pencil

Peter Kuper

Art Director: Peter Kuper
Publication: various (syndicated), 1991   Publishing Company: INX/United Features
This syndicated illustration shows the results of "Collateral Damage," the military term for civilian deaths.
Enamel paint, colored pencil   № 71

Josh Gosfield

Art Director: Paul Davis
Publication: WigWag, November 1990   Publishing Company: Wigwag Magazine Company
Highlighting historical events of the month, this image appeared on the November cover of Wigwag.
Oil on canvas

№ 72

Amahlia Stevens

Art Director: Neville Burtis   Writer: Preston Lerner
Publication: LA Style Magazine, September 1990   Publishing Company: American Express Publishing
"The Drug War vs. The Bill of Rights" featured this image in an article about misconduct at
the Los Angeles Police Department.
Oils, silkscreen, aluminum litho plate   № 73

Maciek Albrecht

Art Director: Nancy Rice   Writer: Sorin Davidovici
Publication: Byte Magazine, June 1990   Publishing Company: McGraw-Hill
"On The Radio" featured this illustration in a series of articles about networking in the computer world.
Acrylic on cardboard   № 74

Maciek Albrecht

Art Director: Nancy Rice   Writer: Tad Mogg
Publication: Byte Magazine, June 1990   Publishing Company: McGraw-Hill
Another article in the series on networking, "Primed for Performance" included this image.
Acrylic on cardboard   № 75

Tom Curry

№ 76

Tom Curry

Art Director: J. Porter   Writer: Judson D. Hale
Publication: Yankee Magazine, September 1990   Publishing Company: Yankee Publishing, Inc.
"What New Englanders Wouldn't Do for Love" featured this illustration.
Acrylic   № 76

Joanie Schwartz

Art Director: Ira Friedlander   Writer: Kelly Brownell, PhD
Publication: American Health Magazine, March 1990   Publishing Company: Readers Digest Magazines
The cyclical nature of weight loss/gain is the subject of "The Yo-Yo Diet."
Oil on c-print   № 77

and non
fiction
technical
vers, complex
srations. Books e
dRens books.

Jonathon Rosen

Designer: Rez Lingen
Author: Jonathon Rosen   Publisher: Poote Press, November 1990
The cover and two inside illustrations from "Intestinal Fortitude," a book on futuristic bio-mechanical sexuality.
Relief photo-engraving on parchment

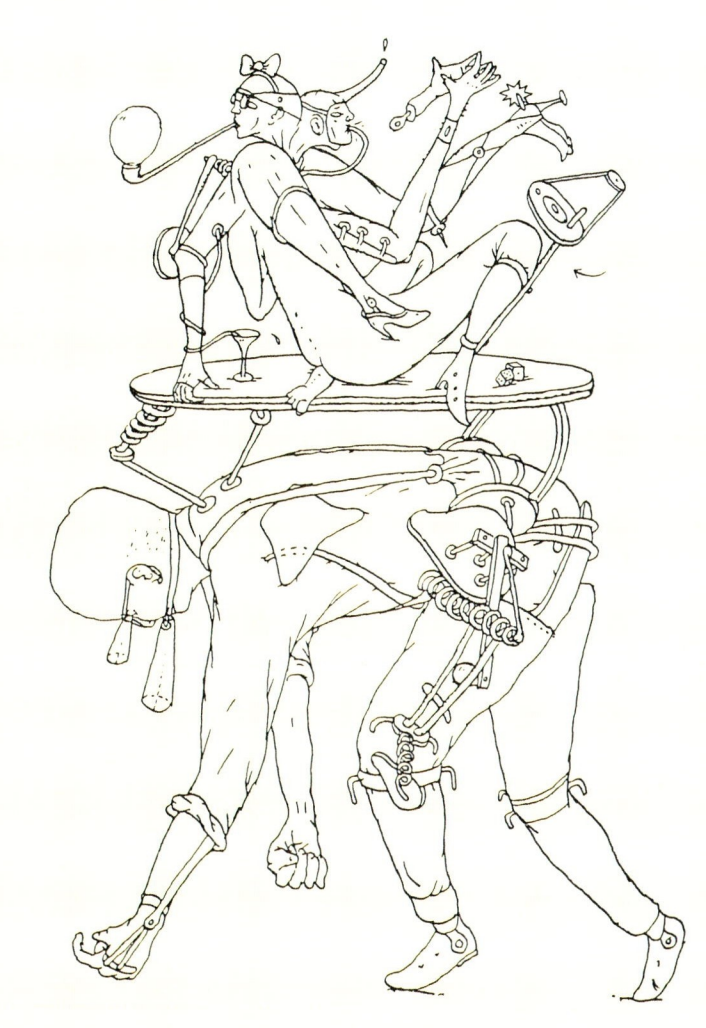

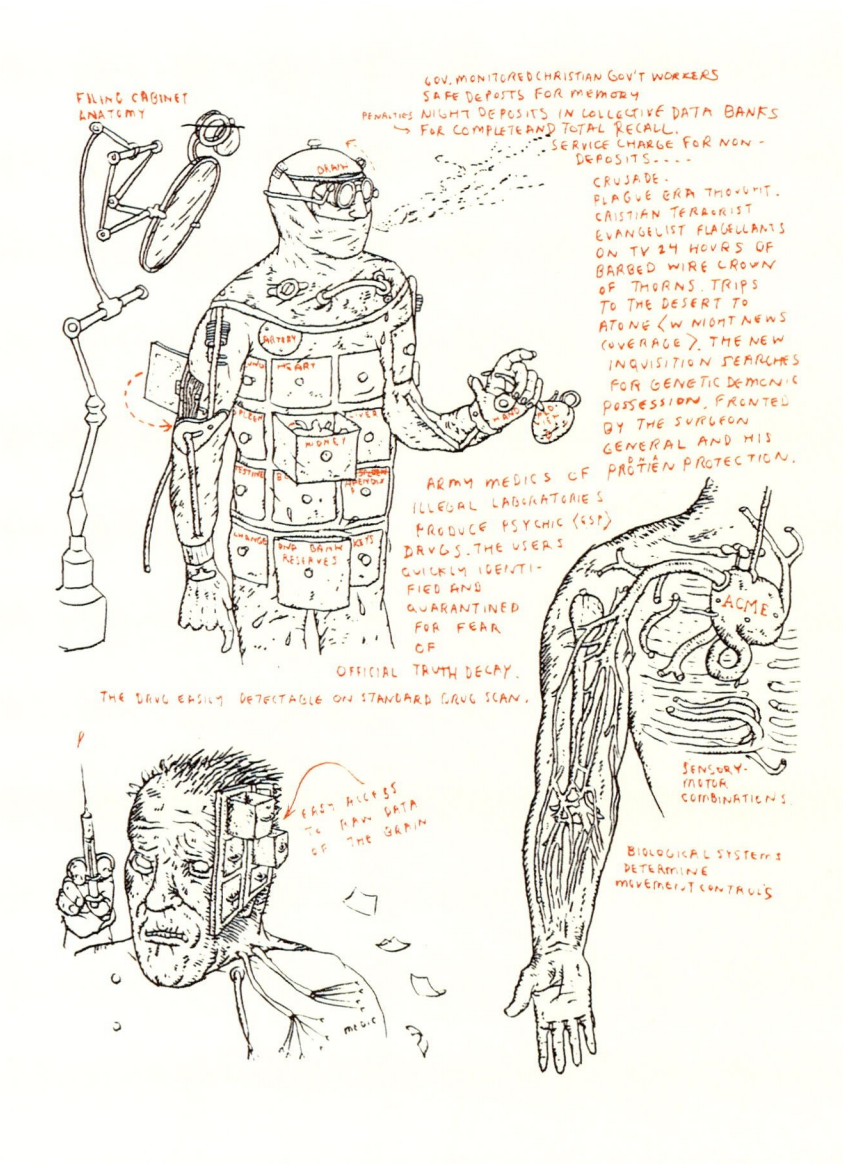

Jonathon Rosen

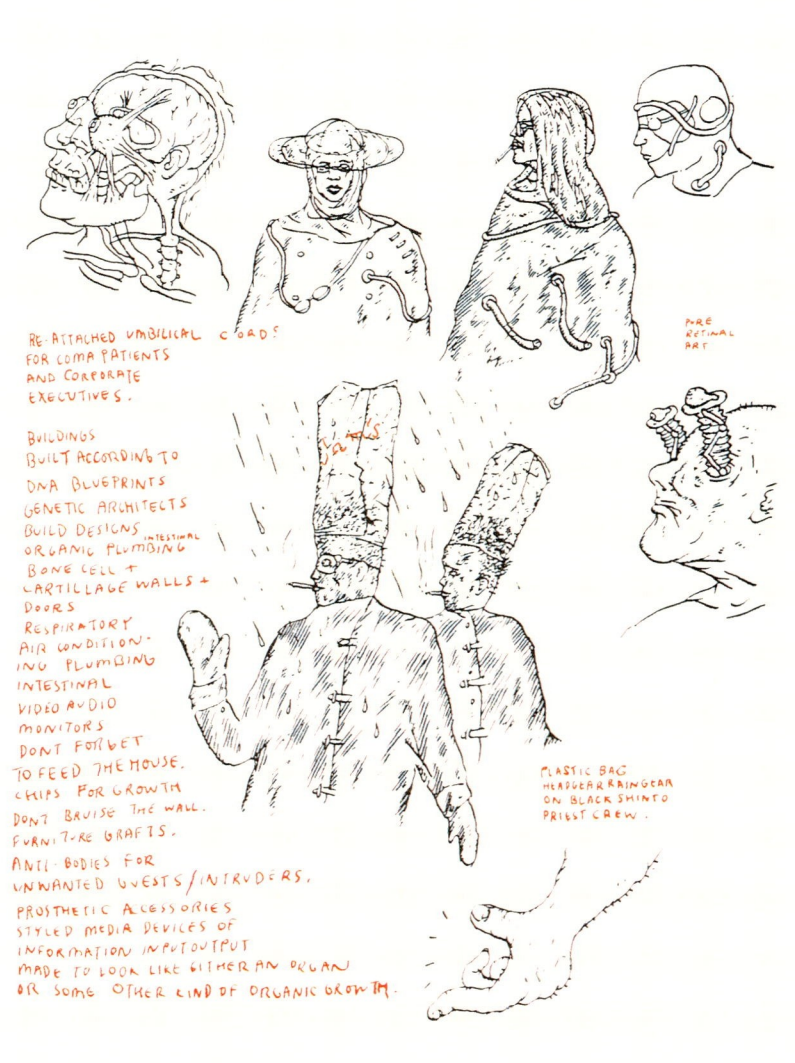

Josh Gosfield

№ 84

Author: Richard Matheson   Editor: Jeff Conner   Publisher: Scream Press, 1990
This illustration appears on the jacket of "Darker," a collection of suspense novels.
Oil and collage on canvas   № 84

Lane Smith

Art Director: Molly Leach
Author: Lane Smith   Editor: Regina Hayes   Publisher: Viking Penguin, 1991
"The Big Pets," a book about a planet where children are small and pets are big,
features this illustration of the Milky Way.

Oils №85

Sara Midda

Art Director: Paul Hansen
Author: Sara Midda   Editor: Sally Kovalchick   Publisher: Workman Publishing Company, October 1990
"Sara Midda's South of France" is the artist's journal/sketchbook, created during a year-long
sojourn in the French countryside.
Watercolors   № 86

Sara Midda

Sara Midda

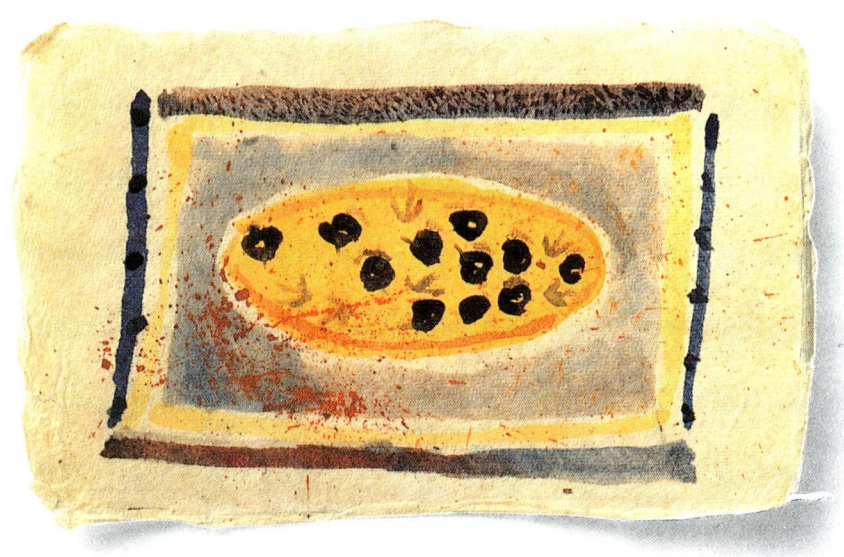

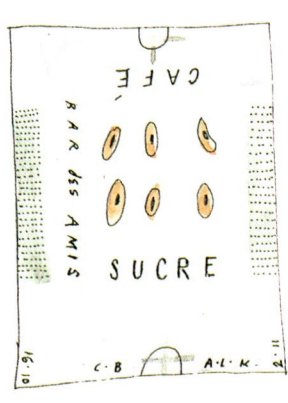

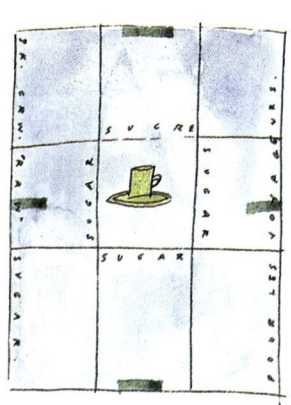
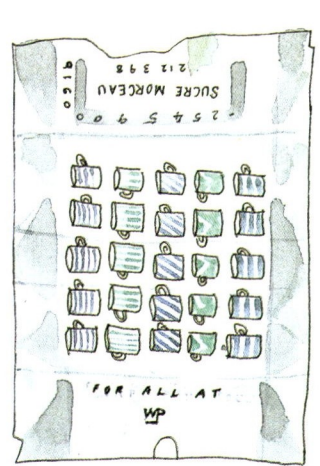

Sara Midda

David Shannon

№ 94

Art Director: Susan Newman
Author: Eugene Ionesco   Editor: Lelia Ruckenstein   Publisher: Paragon House, October 1990
Written at the height of his career, "Fragments of a Journal" is a look at the inner life of the dramatist.
Acrylic

peter Kuper

Author: Upton Sinclair Editor: Wade Roberts Publisher: Berkeley Books/First Publishing, May 1991
In a graphic adaptation of the classic novel "The Jungle," this illustration depicts a riot scene in Chicago's meat-packing plants.
Stencil, enamel, watercolor, colored pencil № 95

Deborah A. Beldring

Art Director: Anne Garner
Author: Herman Melville   Editor: Anne Garner   Publisher: The Bozarts Press, 1990
"The Great Big Picture Book of Great Literature" features this illustration encapsulating the classic novel "Moby Dick."
Charcoal pencil   № 96

Craig Nielsen

Art Director: Anne Garner

Author: James Joyce   Editor: Anne Garner   Publisher: The Bozarts Press, 1990

"A Portrait of the Artist as a Young Man," shown in sixty wordless panels, is also included in "The Great Big Picture Book of Great Literature."

Pen and ink   № 97

Philippe Lardy

Designer: Sheri G. Lee   Editor: Philippe Lardy, Jose Ortega   Publisher: Gin & Comix, March 1990

The front cover of "Gin & Comix."
Ink and PMS colors   № 98

Jose Ortega

This illustration, entitled "Be Dog Bop," is the back cover of "Gin & Comix," a comic book showcasing work by U.S. and European comic book artists.
Scratchboard and PMS colors   № 99

David Sandlin

"Satan Sheets" is featured in the centerfold of "Gin & Comix."

Pastel and ink № 100

Advertis(Consumer, trade and P magazines OR mercha material and supple

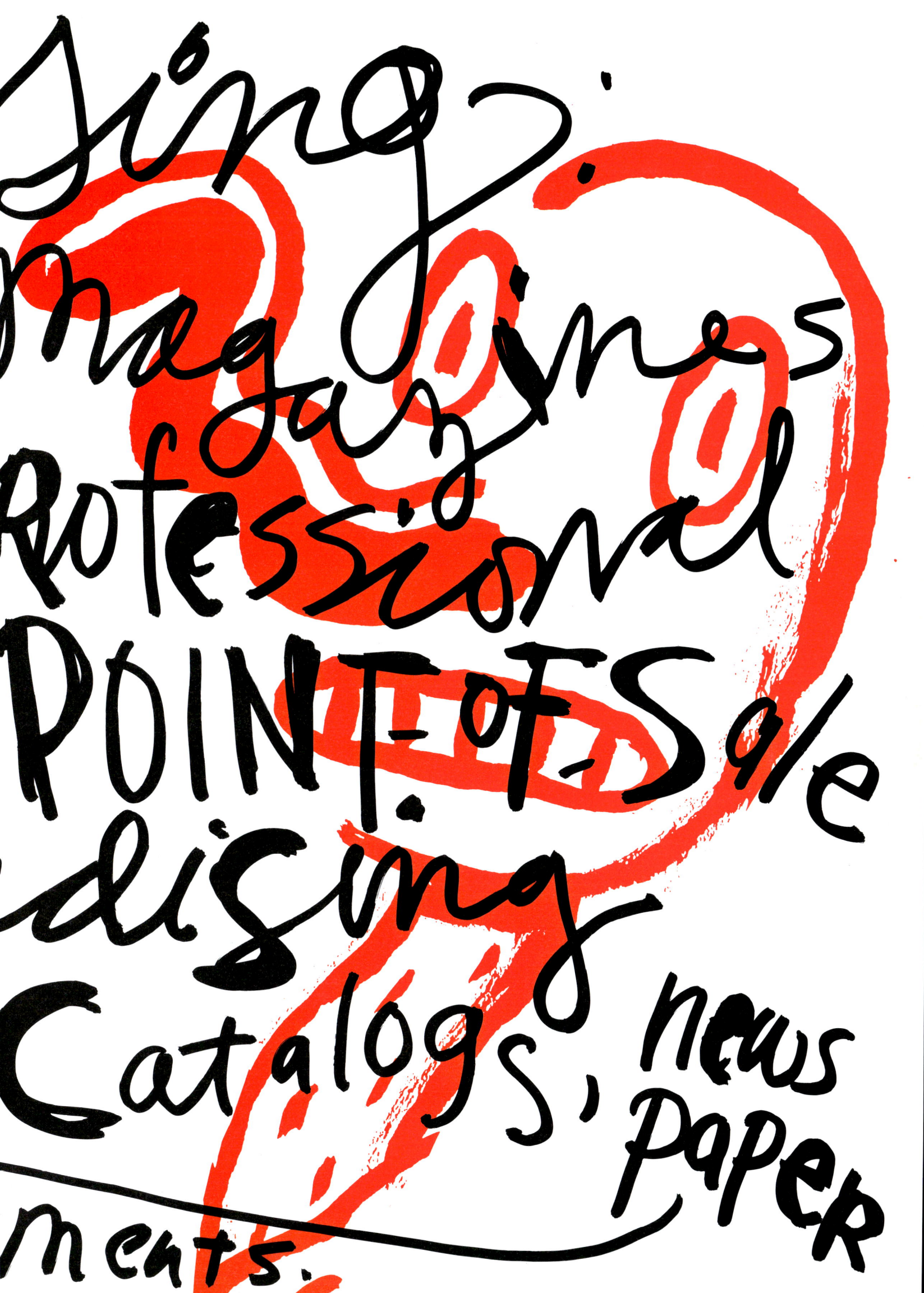

Greg Dearth

№ 104

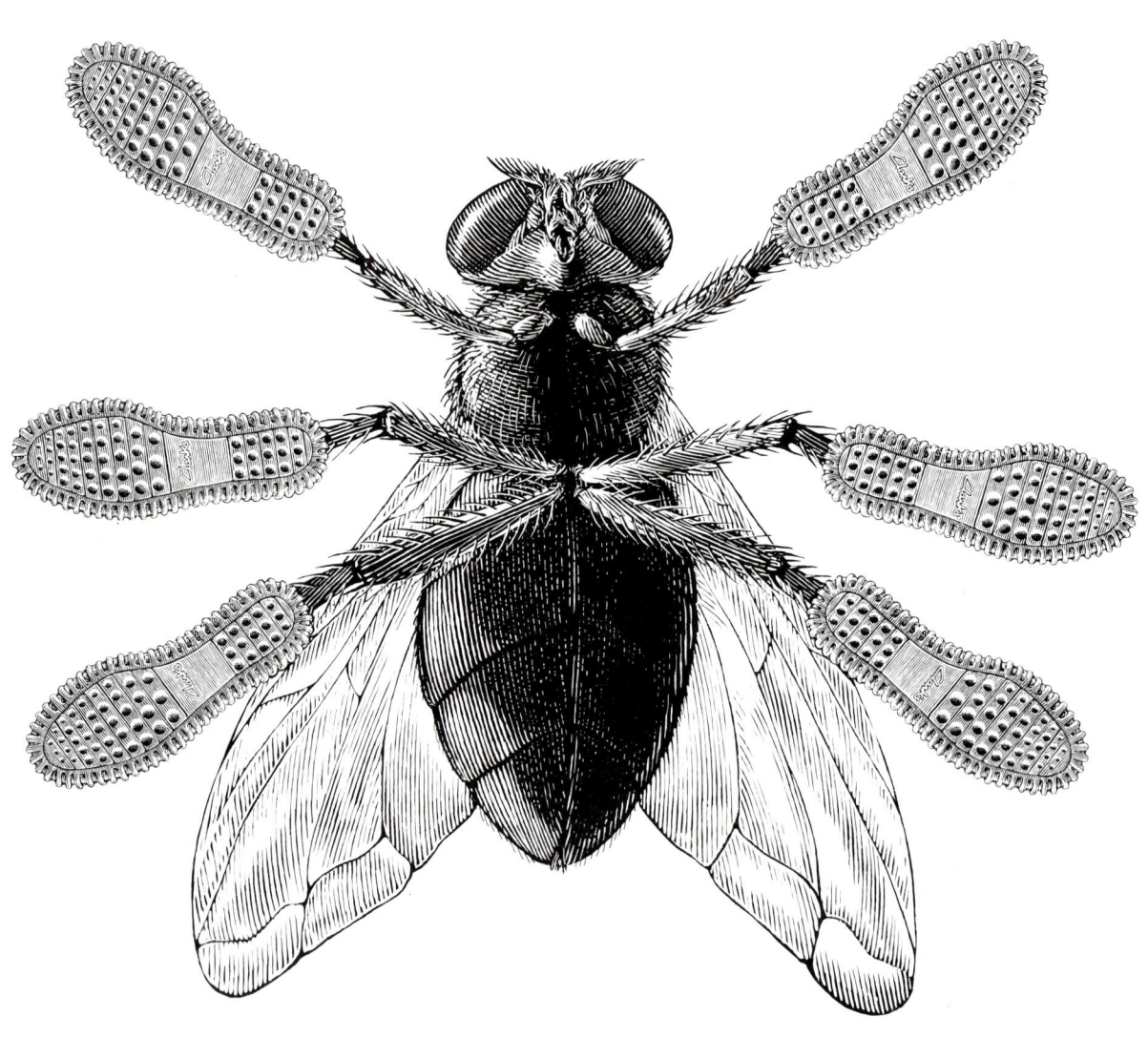

Art Director: Tracy Wong   Agency: Goodby, Berlin & Silverstein   Copywriter: Clay Williams
Client: Clark's of England, June 1990   Publication: Footwear News
A fly wearing shoes was featured in an advertisement for "Big Gripper" footwear.
Scratchboard   № 104

Jessie Hartland

Art Director: Steven Johanknecht   Agency: BNY Advertising   Client: Barneys America, August 1990
One in a series of 20 props produced for display windows, this 3-D illustration
highlights some of the street foods New York is famous for.
Foamcore and acrylics   № 105

Ann Field

Art Director: Clive Piercy   Agency: P.H.D.   Client: Jazz Furniture Gallery, February 1990
These two images were created as part of a campaign reflective of the
1930's style of the furniture available at the gallery.
Chalk pastel   № 106

Ann Field

№ 107

P●l Turgeon

Designer: J●celyne F●urnel   Client: All Quebec Exhibiti●n, Fall 1990
This image was used to promote the annual exhibition of the Association of Illustrators of Quebec.
Ink, gouache, collage, ●il   № 111

Calef Brown

Art Director: Stacy Drummond   Agency: Sony Music   Client: Columbia Records, August 1990
A portrait of the musical artist "Biscuit" was created to promote his new album.
Mixed Media   № 112

James McMullan

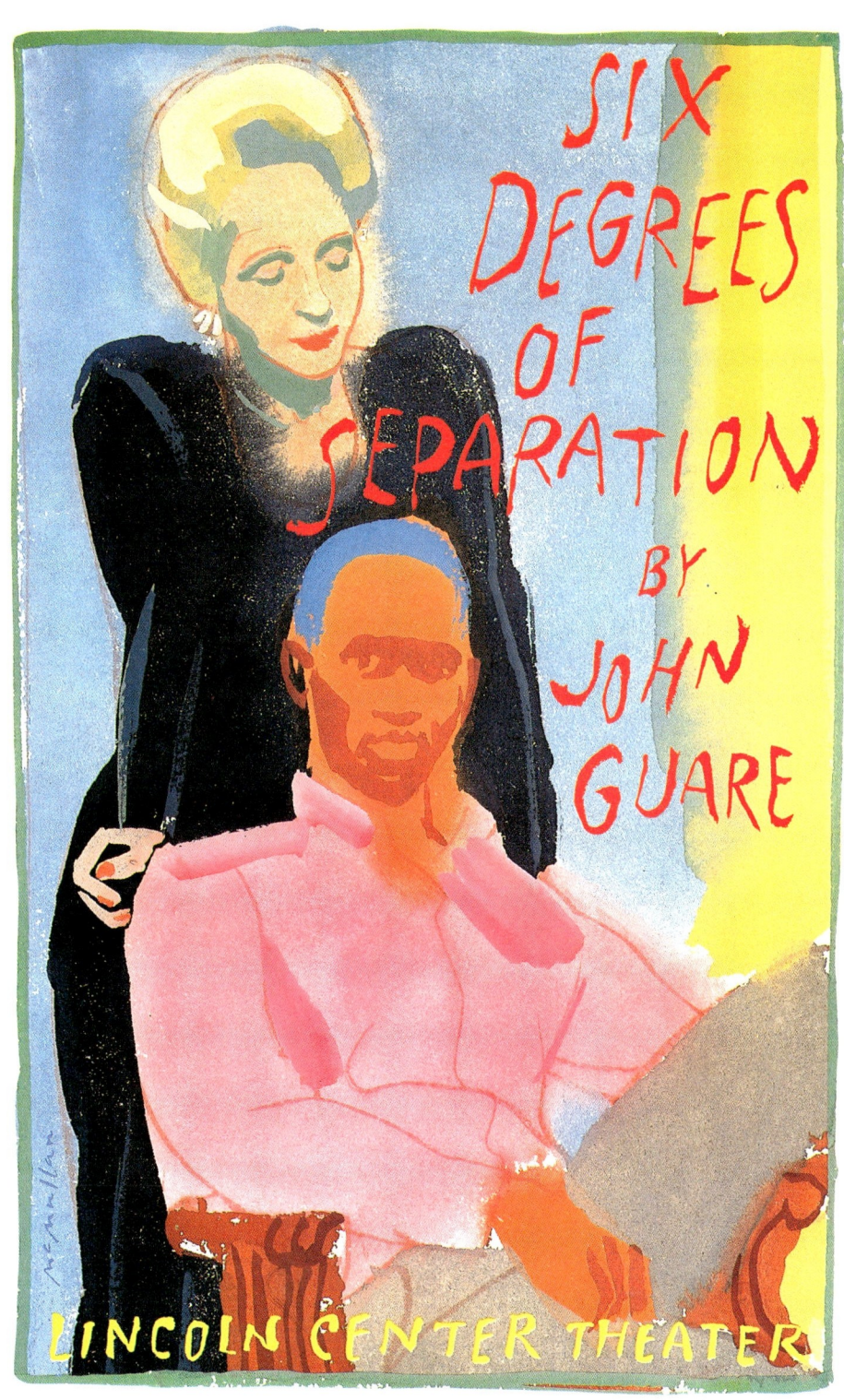

Art Director: Jim Russek
Agency: Russek Advertising   Client: Lincoln Center Theatre, October 1990
The interaction between the two main characters is captured in this theatre poster.
Gouache № 113

Gerald Bustamante

Art Director: Gerald Bustamante   Client: Bicycling West, Inc., June 1990
Created to look like it was painted on the side of a shack, this poster
announces the Rosarito-Ensenada 50 Mile Fun Bicycle Ride in Baja California, Mexico.
Collage, acrylics, spray paint   № 114

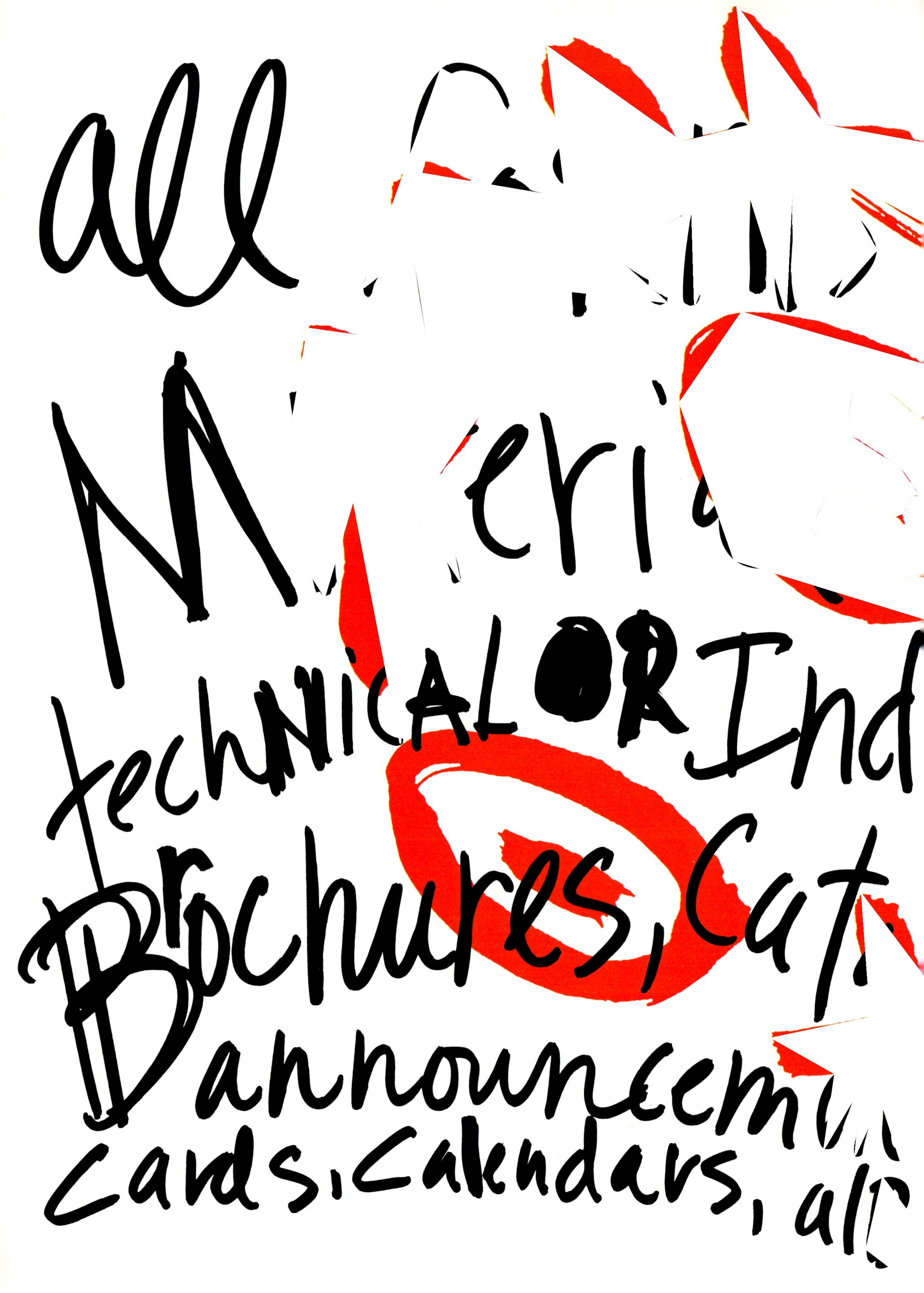

all Material
technICALORInd
Brochures, Cat
Dannouncem
cards, calendars, al

of Promotion: design including strial Literature, egs, direct mail 5, Annual Reports, covers.

Josh Gosfield

Designer: Josh Gosfield   Publisher: Purgatory Pie Press, August 1990
This illustration, printed on bark paper, served as the artist's wedding announcement.
Letterpress №118

Brian Cronin

Designer: Brian Cronin   Publisher: An Post, December 1990
These two images of the Holy Family were created for the Irish national Christmas postage stamps.
Pen and ink, Watercolor   № 119

Perry Farrell and Casey

Designer: Tom Recchion   Publisher: Warner Brothers Records, 1990
This illustration, created by leadsinger Farrell and friend, was used as an album cover for
the group Jane's Addiction.
Mixed Media
№ 120

David Cowles

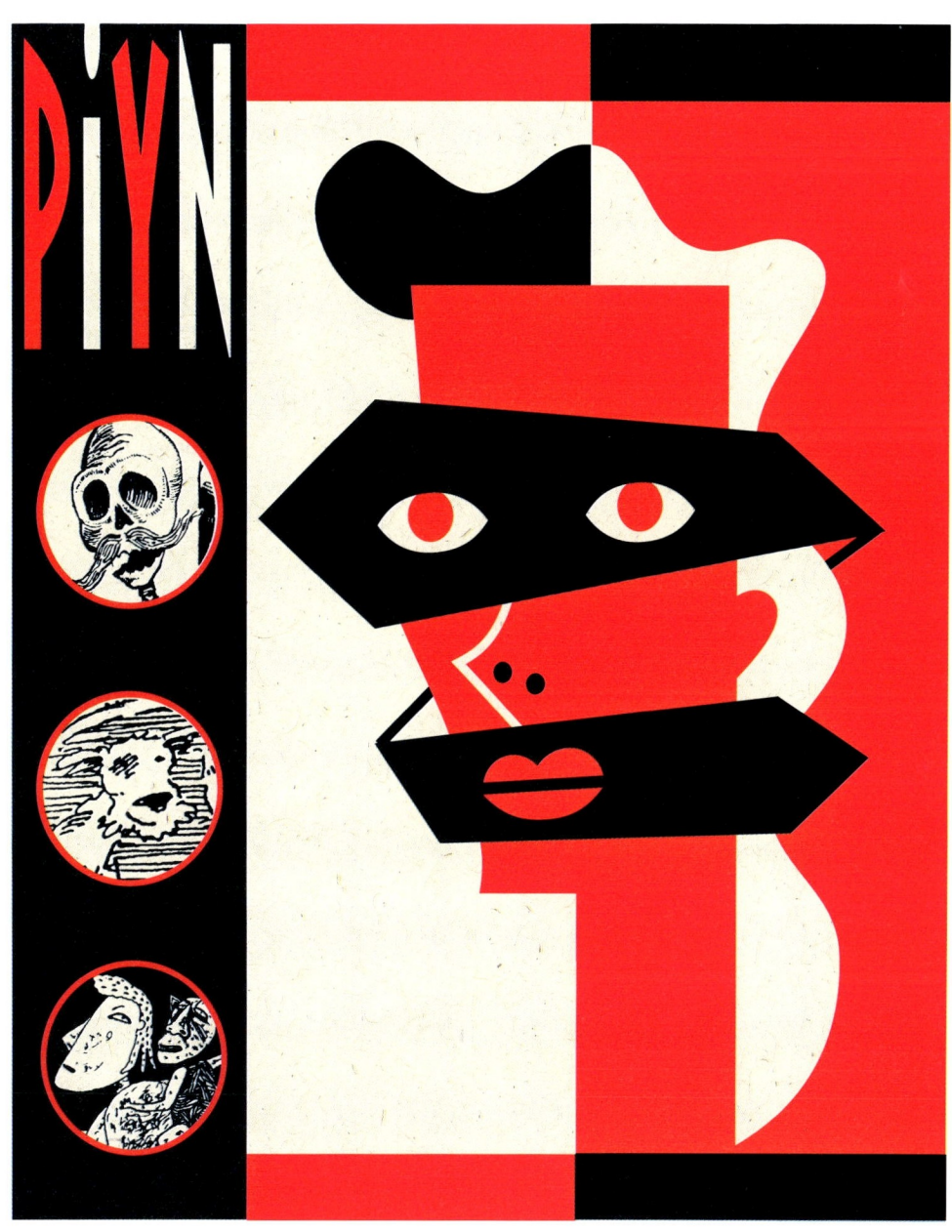

Art Director: David Cowles   January 1991
"People in Your Neighborhood" appeared as a self-promotional booklet, and featured
this image on the cover.
Macintosh IIsi, Aldus Freehand   121

Maria Friske

№ 122

Art Director: David Cowles   January 1991
This comic strip illustrating the lyrics to Neil Young's song, "Rockin' In The Free World"
also appeared in "People in Your Neighborhood."
Pen and ink   № 122

patty Dryden

Art Director: Ria Lewerke   Client: RCA Records, Fall 1990
This illustration was created for the cover of the Bluebird Sampler, a compilation disc of Jazz music.
Oil on glass №124

Paula Munck

Art Director: Cheryl Watson   Writer: Vicky Rossi   Client: Dayton Hudson Department Stores, Spring 1990
To celebrate the arrival of Spring, Dayton Hudson used this illustration on
their store shopping bags.
Gouache and pencil   № 125

Philippe Weisbecker

Art Director: Paul Davis   Designer: Marianna Ochs   Design Group: Paul Davis Studio
Client: Nexus World-Japan, March 1991
This piece on lifestyle and the environment was commisioned by a Japanese housing
developer to appear in their new brochure.
Mixed media, recycled paper

Brad Holland

Acrylic on masonite № 127

Art Director: Jennifer Phillips   Design Group: Barton-Giller   Client: New School for Social Research, 1990
The New School for Social Research used these three illustrations in their brochure.
Acrylic on masonite № 127

Brad Holland

№ 128

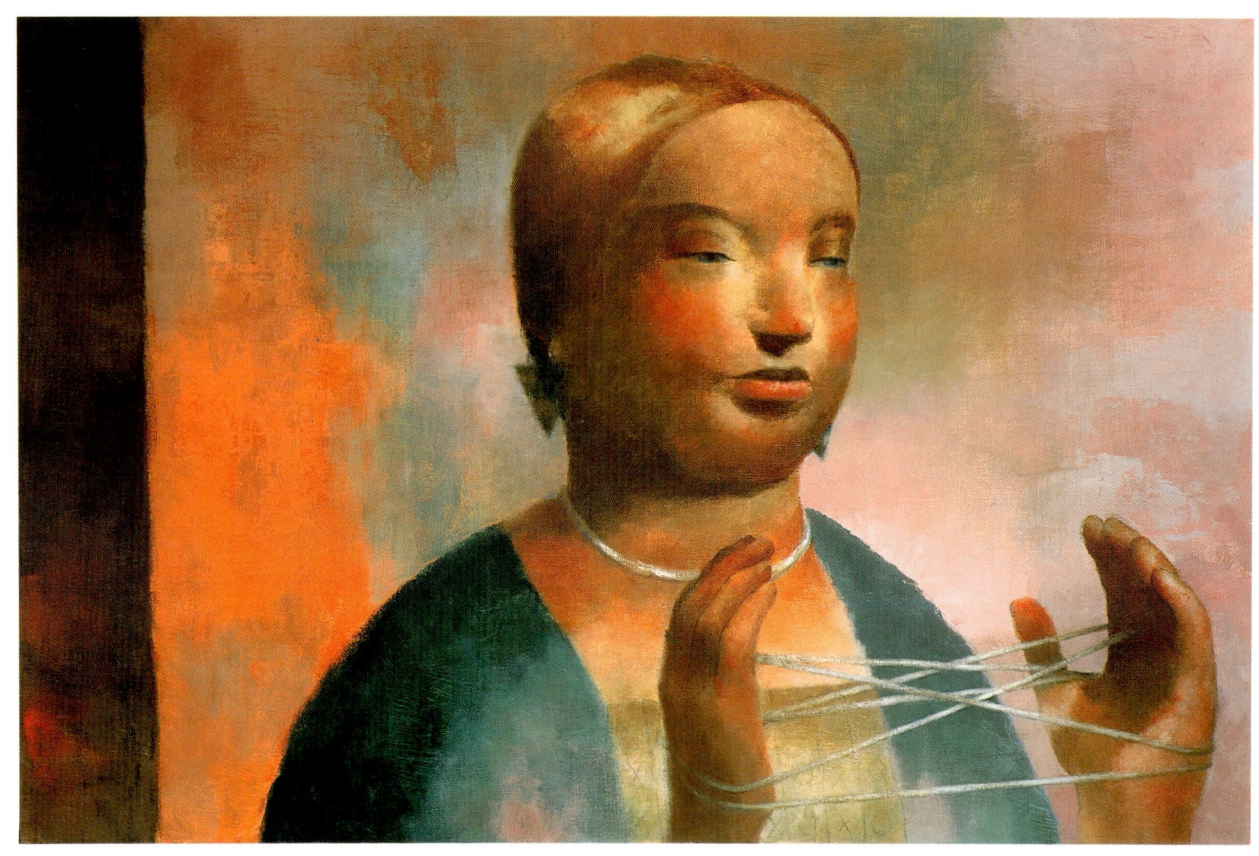

Brad Holland

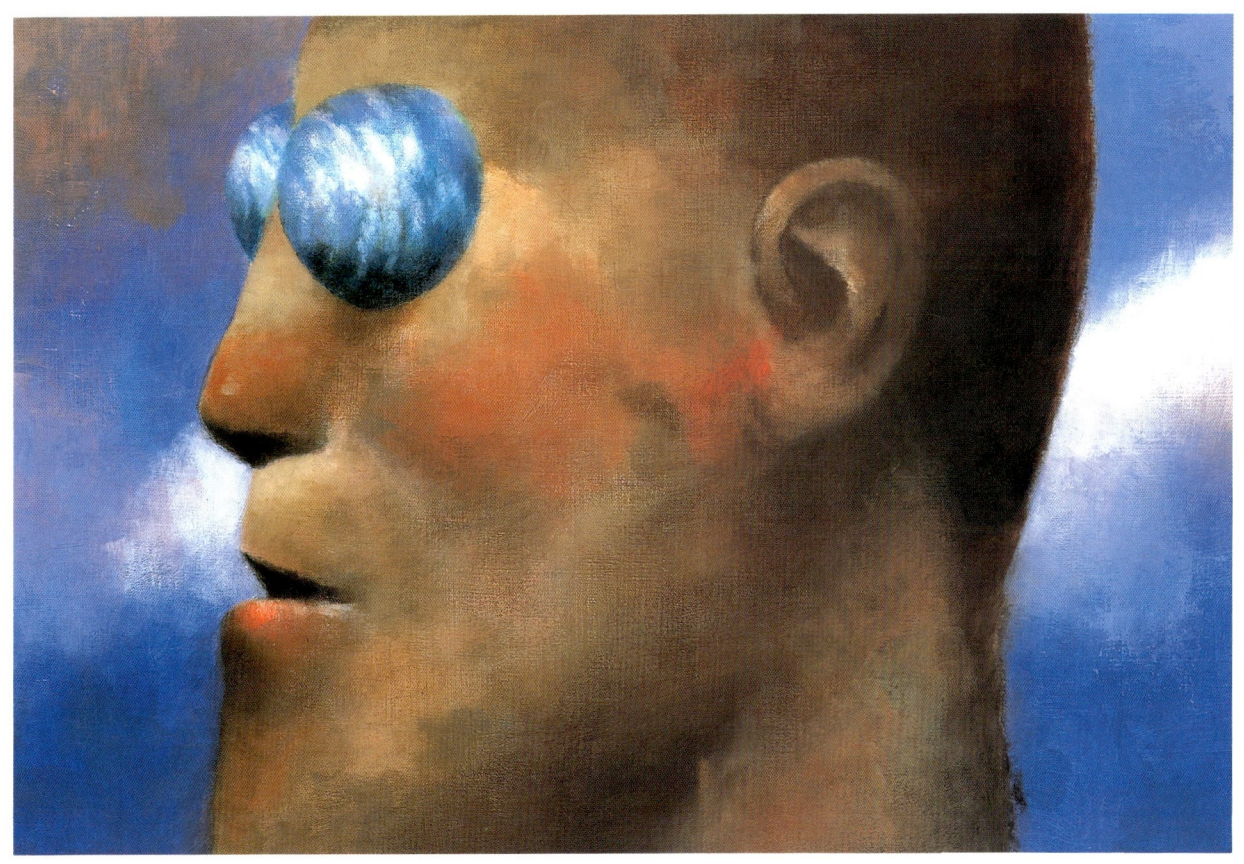

№129

Laura Levine

Art Director: Tommy Steele   Designer: Jeffery Fey   Design Group: Capitol Records Art Department
This portrait of musician Richard Thompson appeared as the album cover for his recording "Rumor and Sigh."
Acrylic on masonite

Michael Klotz

Designer: Michael Klotz   Client: Polygram Records, January 1991
This illustration appeared as an album cover.
Collage, scratchboard

Harry Campbell

Art Director: Harry Campbell
Created for a self-promotional mailer, this illustration appeared in Fall 1990.
Acrylic № 132

Amy Guip

Art Director: Amy Farr   Publisher: Musician Magazine, Spring 1991
Influenced by old playing cards, these five images were commissioned by
Musician Magazine to be used on the cover of the compilation disc "A Little on the CD Side."
Mixed collage

Amy Guip

№ 134

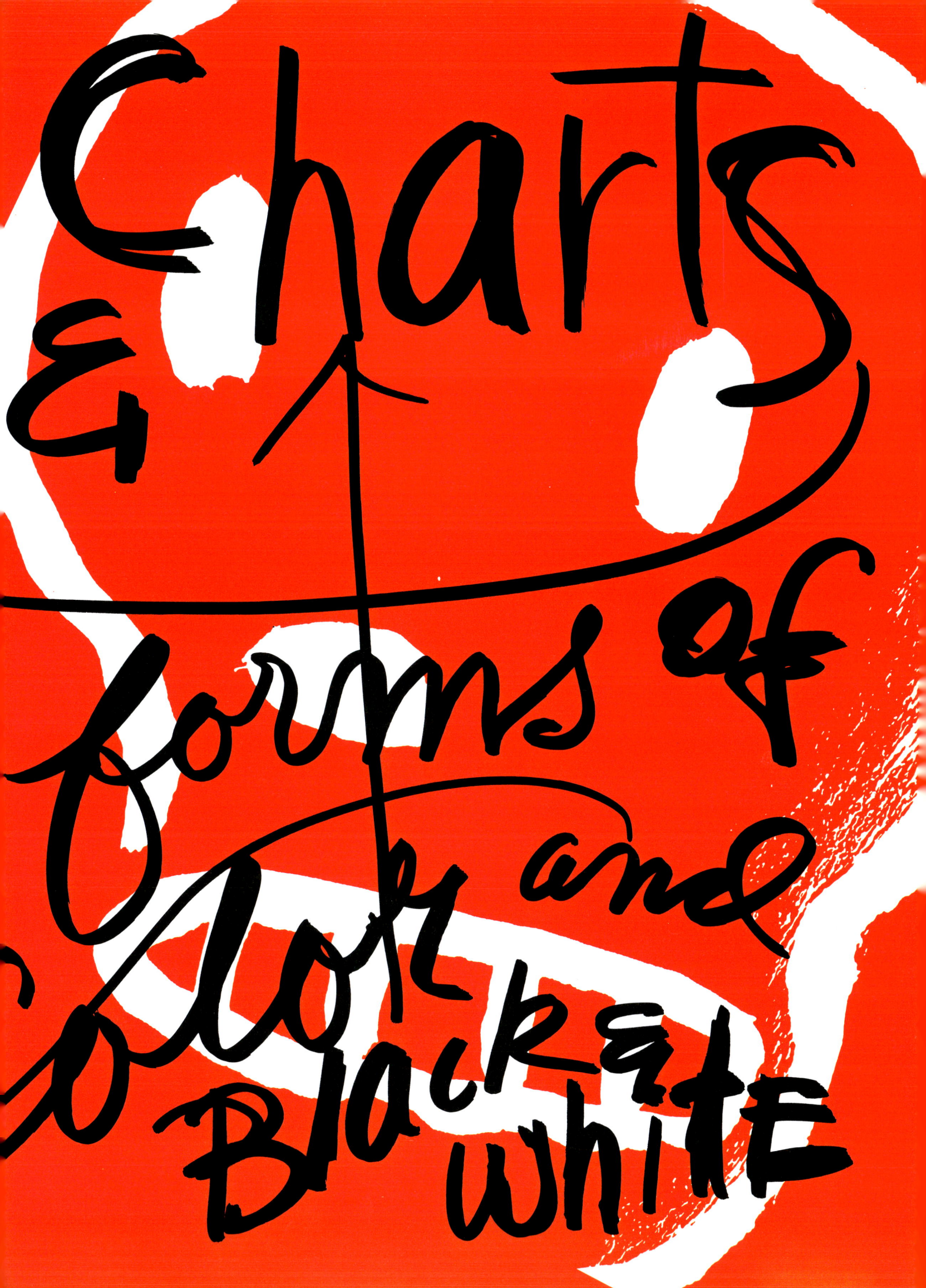

Lane Smith

Art Director: Fred Woodward
Publication: Rolling Stone, April 1990   Publishing Company: Straight Arrow Publishers
In their special Earth Day issue, Rolling Stone featured this map on the title page.
oil, collage   № 141

Istvan Banyaj

№142

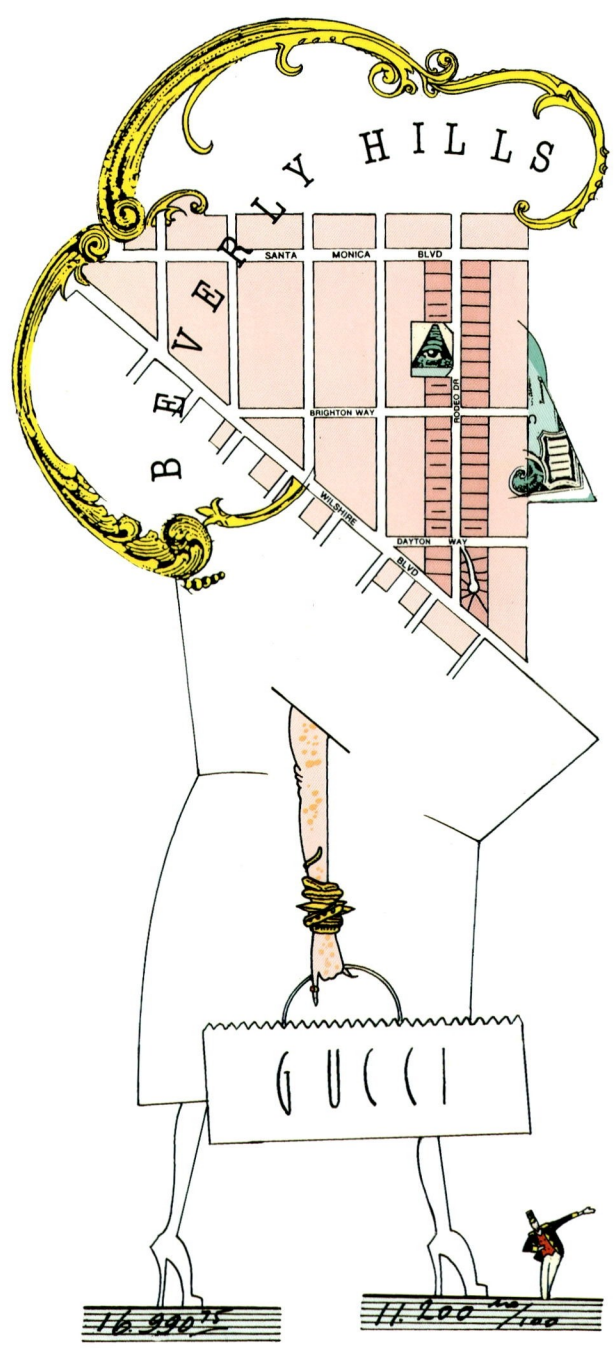

Art Director: J.C. Suares   Design Group: Spade & Archer   Publisher: Gousha/Simon & Schuster
To accompany "Zsa Zsa's Walking Tour of Rodeo Drive," this illustration identifies the shops of Beverly Hills.
Ink, celluloid, cellpaint   №142

Daniel Craig

Art Director: Clifford Selbert   Designer: Linda Kondo   Design Group: Clifford Selbert Design, Inc.
Client: New York Botanical Garden, Spring 1990
This bird's eye view of the Botanical Garden appeared on signs in the garden and also in brochures.
Acrylic № 143

Personal
by Prof
Unpubli
for PRESS

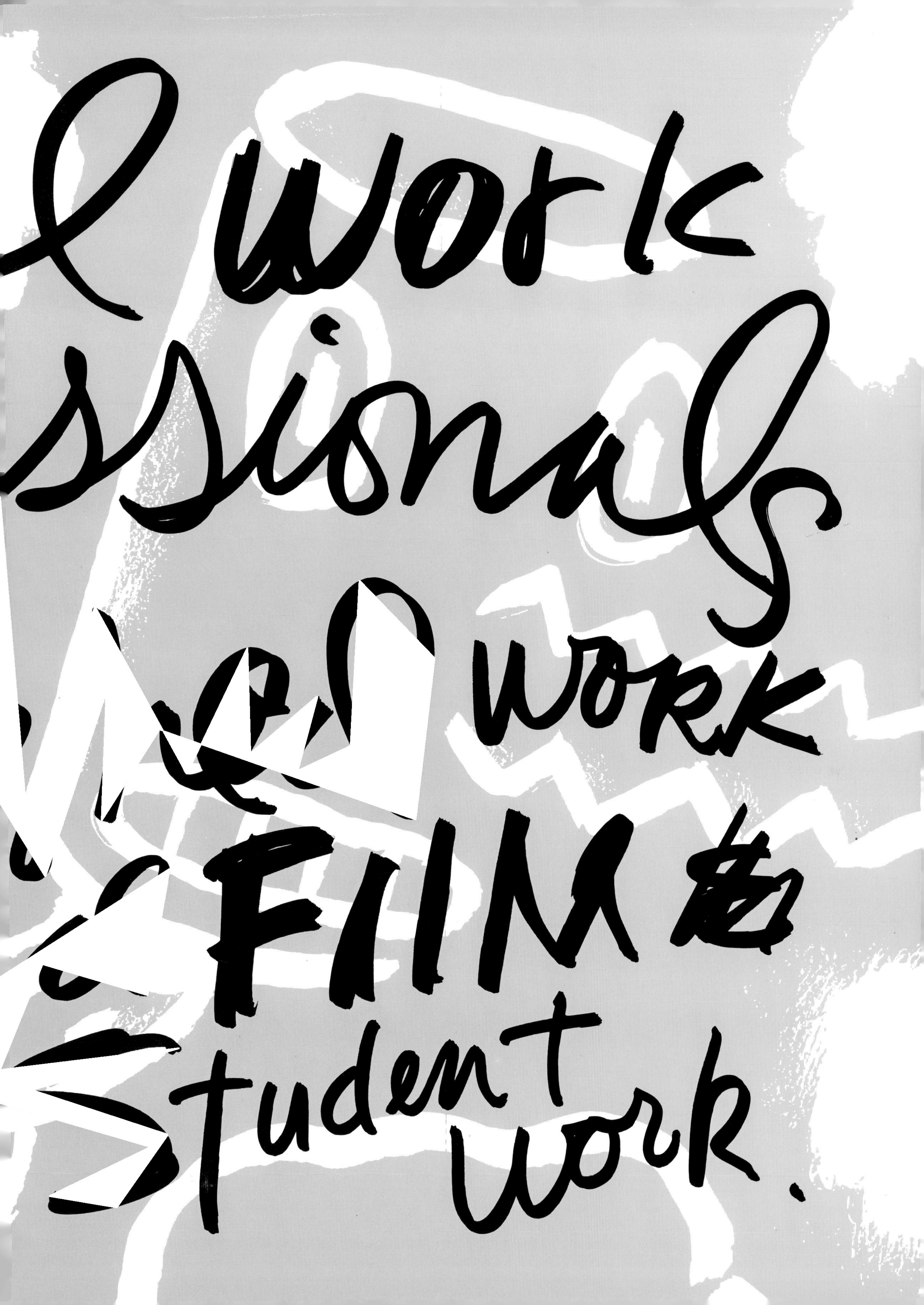

work
ssionals
of work
FILM
Student
work.

Tom Christopher

Acrylic, September 1990. 158

A personal work, "Manhattan Light" focuses on the inner city struggle and the knife-like light of lower Manhattan.

Thomas Webb

One in a series illustrating elementary school memories, "Peter Ate Paste" is based on a childhood acquaintance. Gouache and ink, May 1990.

№ 157

Karen Barbour

Art Director: David Armario   Author: Mario Vargas Llosa
Commissioned but unused, "In Praise of the Stepmother" was created for an article in Esquire Magazine on Mario Vargas Llosa's book.
Gouache, July 1990 · № 147

Gary Baseman

"God Send" is one in a personal series which centered on the themes of ego, sacrifice, and desire. Acrylic and collage, October 1990. №148

Dave Calver

"Bottle-shaped Torso" is part of a series based on a sketch done for a New York Magazine jewelry advertorial. Marker, colored pencil, acrylic, January 1991. №149

Nancy Jakubowski

Thoughts of Alaska and a favorite television program were the catalyst for this untitled piece. Watercolor and colored pencil, Summer 1990.

№ 150

Jack Endewelt

This personal image is one in a series of "Famous Aircraft of the World."
Oil on linen, June 1990.
№ 151

cindy sandro

Based on an earlier assignment, "Fantasy Tea 3-Mystic Moon" is one of three in a series.
Gouache, acrylics, fabric, glue, May 1990. № 152

Mark Ulriksen

Focusing on the how people can be alone when together, "The Unhappy Couple" was created as an experiment using small brushes. Oil, Summer 1990.

№ 153

Karen Barbour

"Head" is a personal piece created for the artist's portfolio.
Ink, pencil, Spring 1990. № 154

Greg Clarke

This untitled personal illustration was created for future self-promotional use.
Oil, December 1990. № 155

David Goldin

The inspiration for "Yoo Hoo Cat" was to give life to a flattened soft drink can.
The image appeared in a group show at the Illustration Gallery called "Cool Cats."
Ink and watercolor, Winter 1990. № 156

Andy Meyer

This personal piece, entitled "Slow Dance,"
is one in a series of explorations into Elvis Presley and his new found fame.
Oil, April 1990. № 159

Jose Ortega

"Azuca' Pa' Mi" was created for self-promotional use in R.S.V.P. The image depicts a working class couple enjoying their after work hours together. Pencil and ink, May 1990.

№ 160

Kouichi Sakumoto

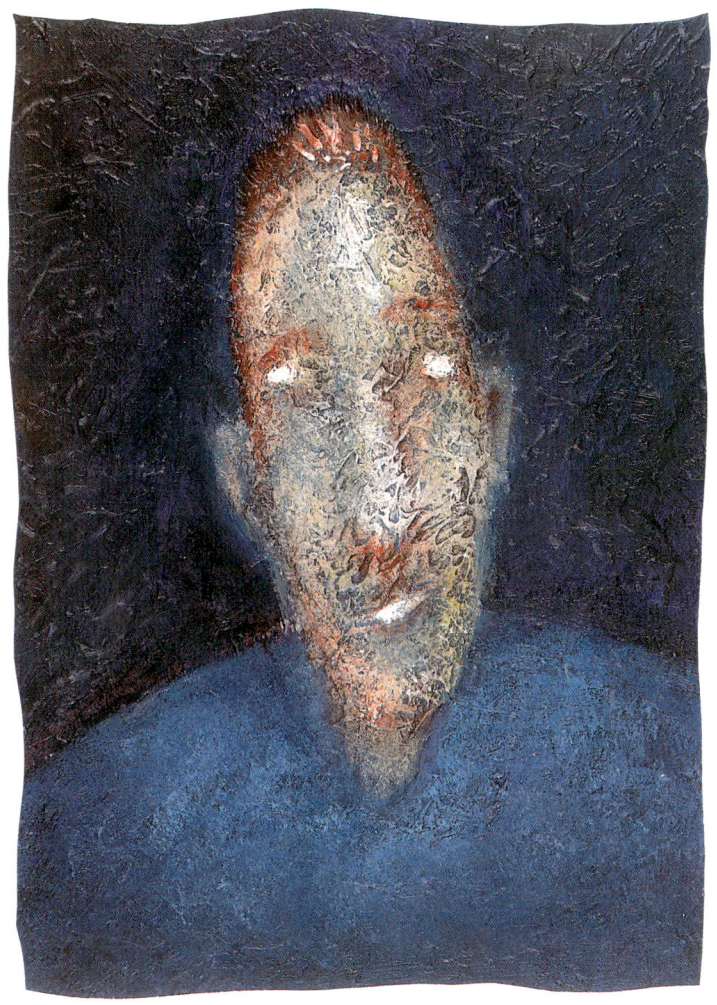

This self-portrait was an assignment for Parsons instructor Warren Linn.
Acrylic, January 1991. № 161

Archil Pichkhadze

"The Boxer" is a personal piece created for the artist's portfolio.
Oil and mixed media, Fall 1990. № 162

Sergio Baradat

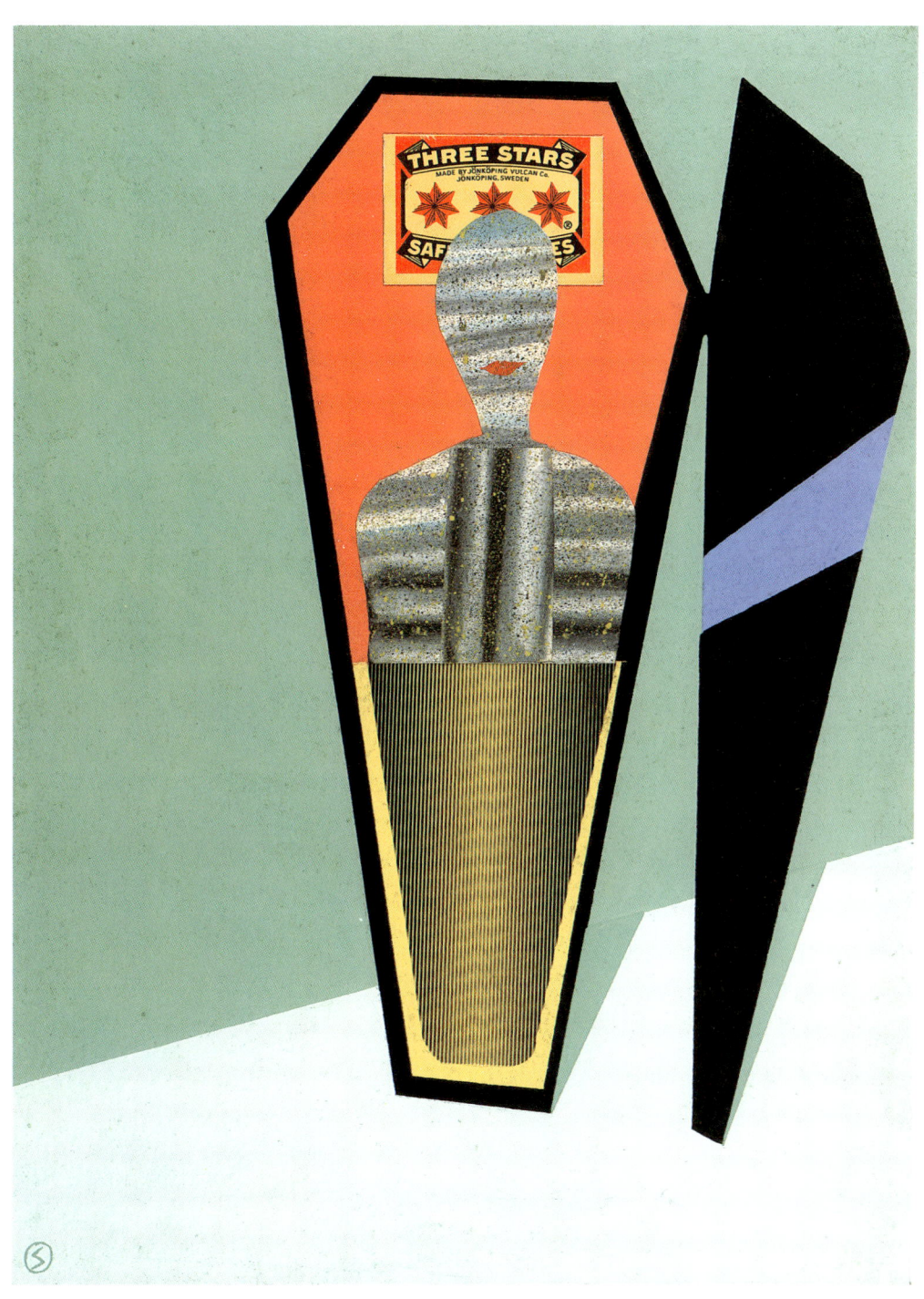

"Three Stars Mummy" is a self portrait of a free-lance illustrator on a bad day. Gouache and collage, January 1991.

Peter Vahlefeld

"Be My Valentine" is a personal political work.
Color xerox, acrylic, oil, January 1991. № 164

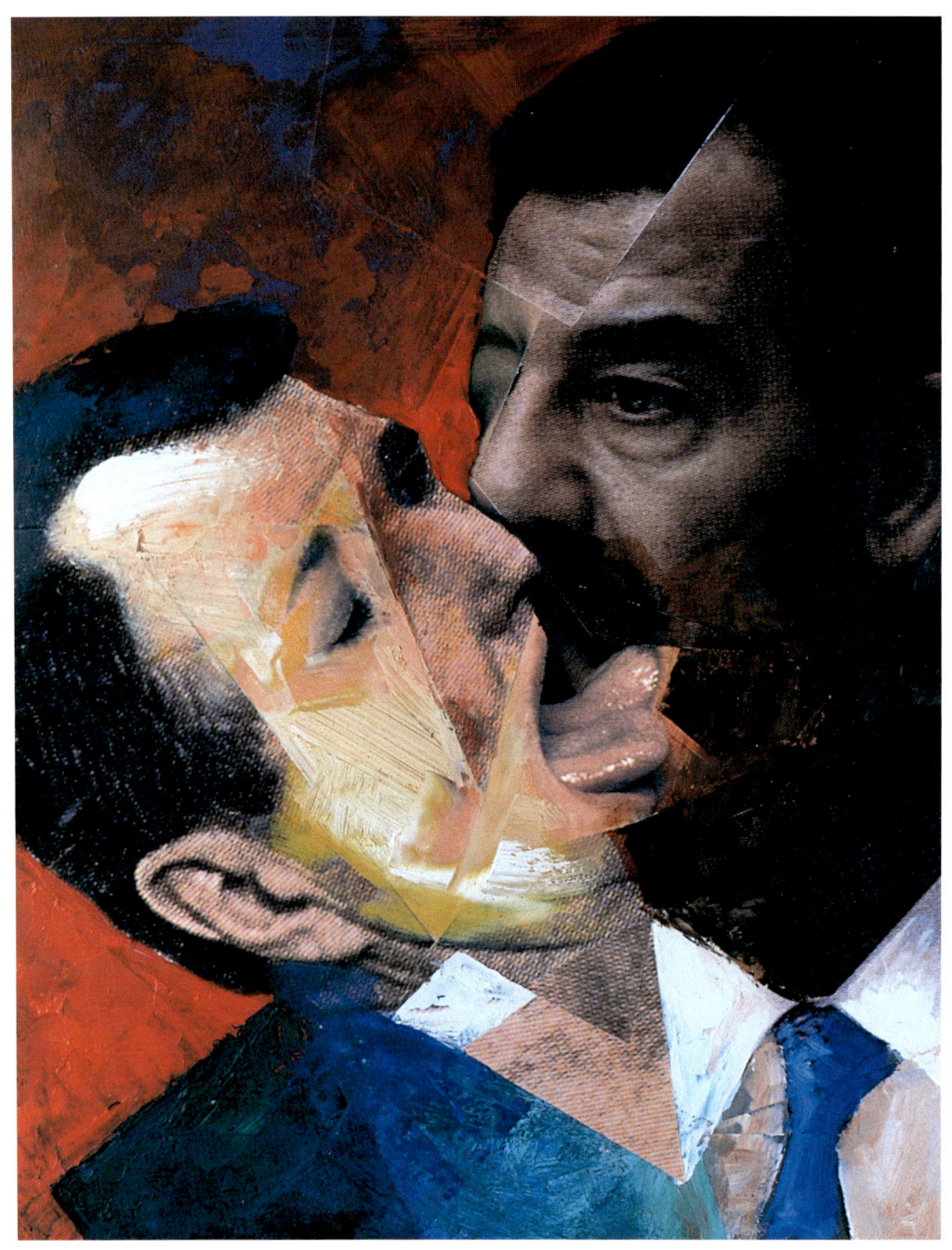

Barry Blitt

Gershwin's "Piano Concerto in F" inspired this personal work entitled "George Gershwin and Hangers-on." Watercolor and ink, November 1990.

Don Sullivan

"Moonlight Mow" is a personal work
concerning a miscommunication between father and son about when to mow the lawn.
Colored pencil, June 1990.

Ruth Marten

Art Director: Fred Woodward
This portrait of rock star Sting was commissioned but unpublished by Rolling Stone Magazine.
Gouache and egg tempera, February 1991. № 167

Advertising
Television
content and
documentary
and promotional
kinds. Music

8 in television, including titles, features, & Educational, films of all videos. computer Graphics.

Mark Marek

Artist/Designer: Mark Marek   Animator: Chris Goldsmith   Director: Lidia Przyluska
Art Director: Drew Takahashi   Producer: Phyllis Adams
Agency/Client: Elektra Records   Music Composition: John Linnell, John Flansburgh
"They Might Be Giants" is a 2-1/2 minute music video about New York City and its inhabitants.
Video animation and 3-D models were used to illustrate
the song lyrics.

Henry Selick

"Slow Bob" is a test film for an experimental animated series.

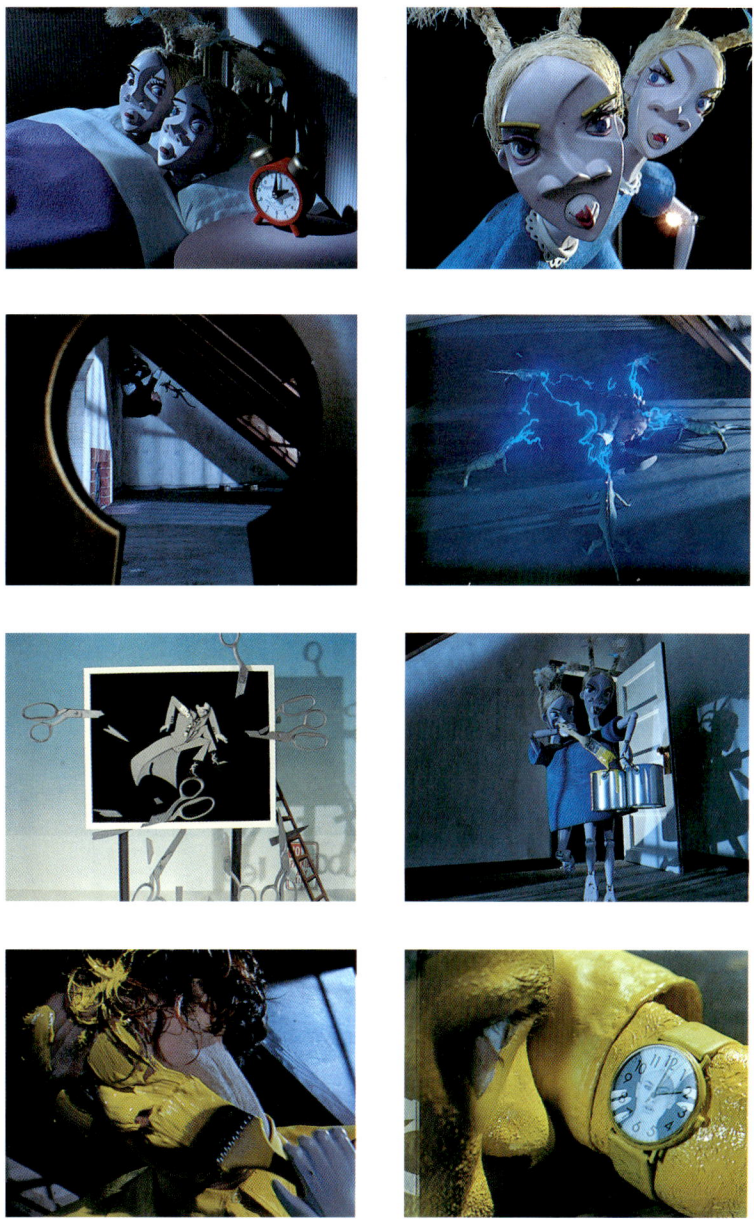

Artist/Designer/Director: Henry Selick   Animators: Eric Leighton, Trey Thomas, Owen Klatte
Art Directors: Ron Davis, Henry Selick   Producer: John Payson
Agency/Client: MTV Networks   Production Company: Selick Projects   Music Composition: The Residents
"Slow Bob" is a test film for an experimental animated series.
Many animation techniques were combined with a live actor to create this
5 minute short.

special Projects

Walter Sipser

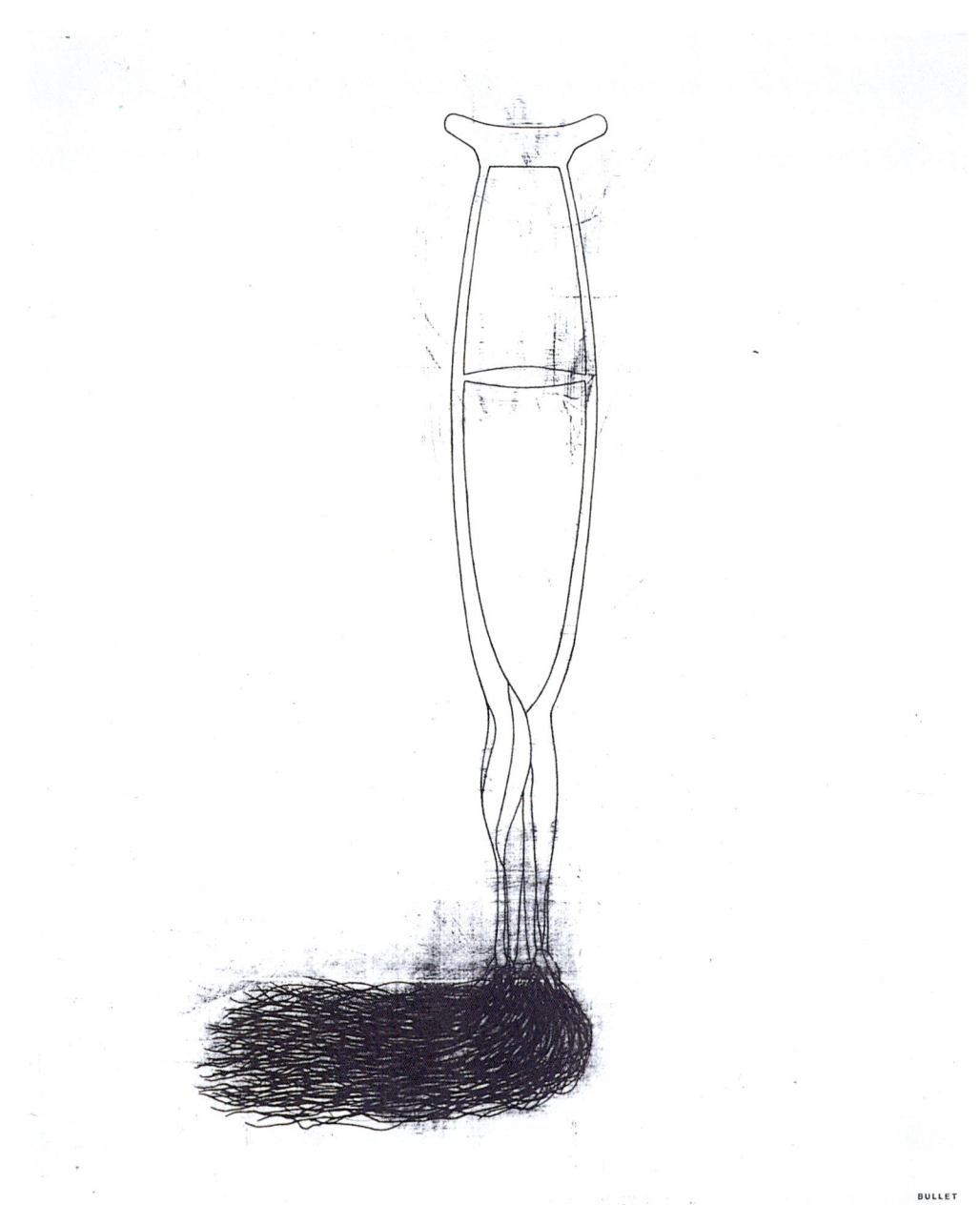

BULLET

Special Project Book (6 images)

Authors: Andrew Castrucci, Nadia Coen, Frank Morales Editors: Andrew Castrucci, Nadia Coen, Frank Castrucci
Publisher: Bullet: An Urban Artists' Collaborative, 1990
Various Media

Part of the New York City street project "Your House Is Mine," this image depicts dependence, human frailty, healing, and regeneration.

pencil

№174

Eric Drooker

The crackdown by transit police on the homeless living in New York's subways is the subject of this piece.

Betzaida Concepcion

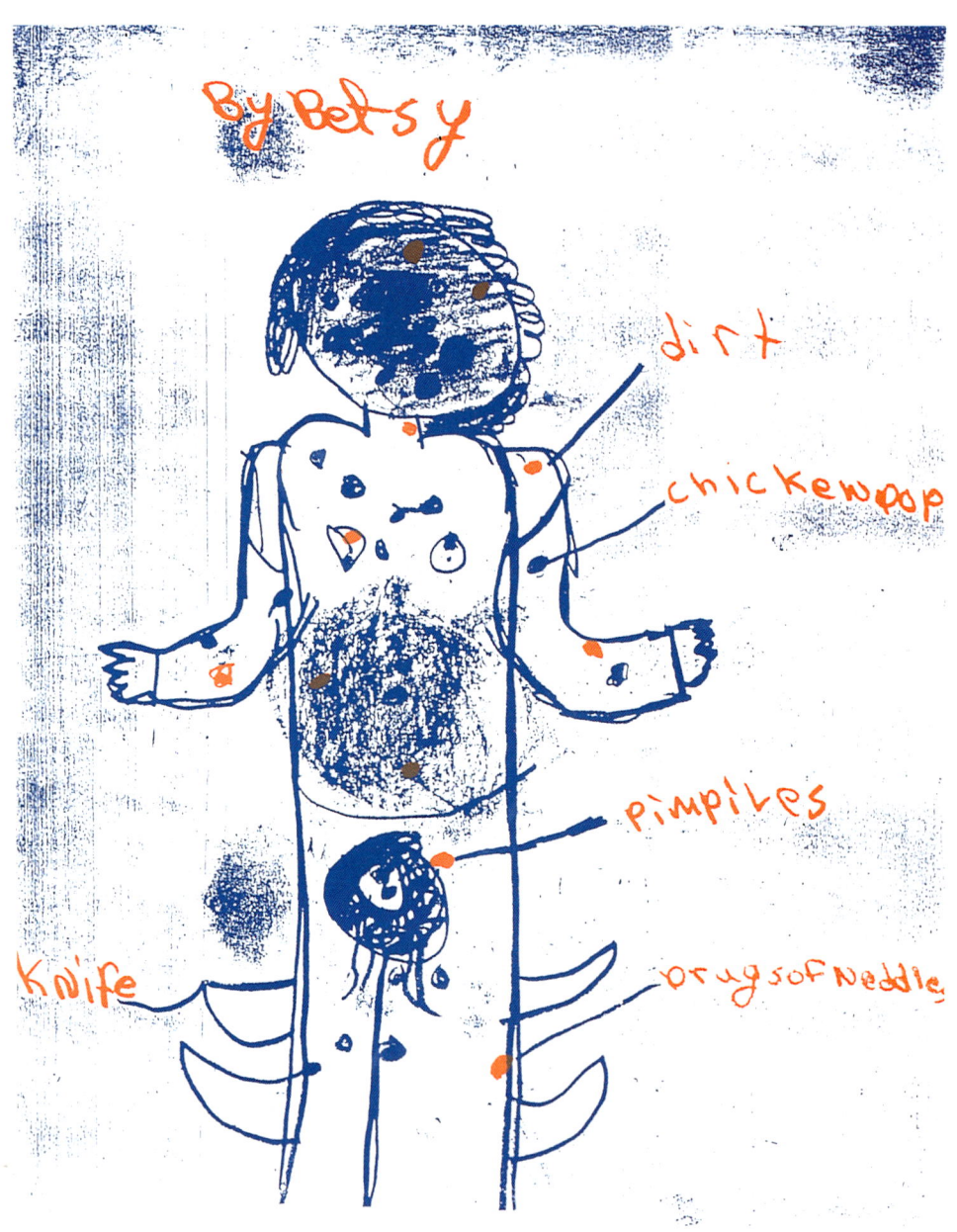

Drawn by an 8 year-old girl, this image depicts a woman she knew at the crack house where she lived on New York's Lower East Side.
Colored pencil

David Wojnarowicz

This illustration reflects the "New World Order" at home.
Collage, charcoal, markers, xerox

Sabrina Jones

One of two images in a series, this work shows a homeless man breaking down a boarded-up door to seek shelter. Stencils, spray enamel

Anton Van Dalen

Documenting the homeless of his neighborhood, the artist created this image for "Your House Is Mine."
Stencil, spray enamel № 179

continued from page 7

the last ten years, the work of some of today's great American illustrators does have distinctive characteristics which brand it "American." The darkly introspective work of Brad Holland and Matt Mahurin contrasts sharply with the more lyrical and gregarious images from Milton Glaser and James McMullan. The graphic styles of Seymour Chwast and RO Blechman are a counterpoint to the imaginative complexities of Marshall Arisman's work.

What marks it out from the rest is that — for me — it is all "American." Not "All-American," but very much a reflection of the multi-faceted American psyche.

There are, of course, many talented European illustrators working in America, whose exceptional gifts we honour year by year. But the people who came to the surface as I sifted through hundreds of images from the last ten years, are the true projectors of the current American style of illustration.

The jury sits in judgement

Our first jury — Ronn Campisi of the Boston Globe, Rudy Hoglund of TIME Magazine, John Macfarlane of Saturday Night Magazine in Toronto, the Dallas-based designer Woody Pirtle, Henrietta Condak of CBS Records, the West Coast designer Gordon Mortensen, Kerig Pope of Playboy in Chicago, Louise Fili of Phantom Books in New York and Hans Teensma of Rocky Mountain Magazine in Denver — made up the group which set the standards for others to live up to, and subsequently improve on.

And our first publishing event set a style we have tried to continue since.

It took the form of a weekend in New York, during which distinguished speakers such as Milton Glaser discussed important aspects of American illustration, and several artists opened their studios to those who had come to the city to celebrate "American Illustration."

In the years since then, we have welcomed the likes of Ralph Steadman, Maurice Sendak, Tomi Ungerer, Fluck & Law of "Spitting Image," the animator Richard Williams and The Thunder Jockeys as guest speakers, while the studio visits have been continuously popular.

One of our most bizarre encounters occurred when Jean-Paul

Goude flew into New York by Concorde to speak at one of our events. I had spent several hours rehearsing with Malcolm McLaren when, two minutes before we were ready to start, Jean-Paul refused to speak to the 500 or so people who had come to hear him. When he asked if he could sit in the audience instead, I said: "No. You must either speak or leave." So he left. And flew home by Concorde. How Malcolm and I managed to re-work our presentation in time, I'll never know!

The goals for the future

Now, after ten years, "American Illustration" stands at a crossroads.

We have broken the Society of Illustrators' grip on American illustration.

We have encouraged a younger generation of illustrators by accepting their student work, just as Sue Coe had her work accepted by "European Illustration" while she was still at London's Royal College of Art. And we have seen these people go on to make successful careers as American illustrators.

We have set and maintained our overall standards of excellence.

And we have gone some way towards defining the true character of American illustration.

Now I would like to see us follow in the continuing footsteps of "European Illustration." For what I started in 1974 as a series of annuals has grown to become the "European Illustration" Centre in Hull.

Here, in an ancient English city once famous for its dominance of the North Sea fishing industry and always for its historic links with Europe's trade, we have established an active centre for the study and development of every aspect of European illustration.

This is my goal for America. The great heritage which "American Illustration" is helping to build needs a centre where it can develop, where young people can see the best of the work created over the last decades, and where the spirit of "American Illustration" can inspire all those who seek the standards of excellence we have always upheld.

American beginnings: from the left, Marshall Arisman, Julian Allen, Edward Booth-Clibborn, Steve Heller, and Robert Priest get their heads together over the embryonic "American Illustration". Ten years on, the pursuit of excellence continues.

American celebrations: The first "American Illustration" Graphic Arts Weekend was held at Parsons, in New York City. Milton Glaser (centre) shared his creative passions and imaginative ideas with guests at the opening seminar. With him, in expansive mood later on, are Judy Fendelman and Edward Booth-Clibborn.

Edward Sorel's illustrations always seem to capture the essential vitality and drama of life. Here, in an image art directed by Mary Shanahan for Gentleman's Quarterly, he brilliantly evokes a passionate moment from the turbulent discord between Zelda and F. Scott Fitzgerald, brought on by Fitzgerald's use of Zelda's diary for his novel, "Tender is the Night." All the movement and energy in this drawing forces you to focus on the fire between Scott and Zelda's eyes, and then to fix on the diary.

Blechman's style must be one of the most copied in the world. His innocent figures living in a troubled world have been plagiarised by countless illustrators and, more recently, numerous animators. Here, in a work from 1987, his delightful touch breathes light-hearted enjoyment into a poster for the Leaf Peeper classical concert series in upstate New York.

№ 183

No selection from "American Illustration" would be complete without a work by BRAD Holland. His ability to see inside a subject, and use his unique wit to reveal some of its inner truths, is extraordinary. In this drawing, commissioned for The NEW YORK TIMES magazine for an article entitled "The Rush to DeRegulate," he cleverly exposes the notion that CORPORATISM is quietly unravelling itself.

MARSHALL ARISMAN has been a leading light in "AMERICAN illustration" since its inception. His complex images have always provoked new ways of seeing things. Here, in a work commissioned by TIME magazine for an article entitled "The Curse of Violent Crime," he pulls no punches and uses all his SKILLS to attack both the subject and our perception of it.

I have been an admirer of Matt Mahurin's work since I first saw any of it. In the TEN years since then, his ideas and technical abilities have developed to such an extent that I think I can fairly claim that he is one of America's most gifted and original Illustrators. Not everyone will like his work. But then, the darker side of humanity is not always easy to deal with. This work was commissioned for an article on animal liberation groups, published in Rolling Stone in 1988.

Seymour Chwast's work always seems to bring out the lighter side of life, And to see it in a sharply Ironic light. This illustration, commissioned for Frankfurter Allgemeine in October 1986, was conceived by Seymour, and shows us in a playful way how much like our pets we often get to look. The graphic qualities of his work often show an incisive and penetrating mind at WORK.

№ 185

No matter what medium Milton Glaser may be working in, his illustrations always spring from the page with the sheer force of originality. Here, in a work for a poster commemorating the Book-of-the-Month Club's sixteenth anniversary, he captures all the delights of the pleasures of reading, and yet never intrudes on its essentially private quality. His own delight in life is, for me, a feature of much of his work.

I couldn't possibly have made this selection and left out the work of "RAW." This extraordinary magazine of avant-garde comics and graphics has been one of the highlights of the last decade. In this illustration, Art Spiegelman encapsulates many of "RAW's" characteristics in a single, complex image, created for "READ YOURSELF RAW," a book compiled from the magazine's first three issues.

№ 186

This is so beautiful I could have it on my wall. James McMullan is such a wonderful draughtsman, with such versatility and variety in his styles. He is also a passionate exponent of illustration, believing in its value and its contribution to life. For me, his work evokes ideas about the innocent pleasures of life, even when he's dealing with comparatively serious subjects. Here he is celebrating an auction held by the Friends of the Hampton Library, to benefit the library's funds.

From "European Illustration 74"

Look through this book and you will see work of an amazingly high standard of creativity and craftsmanship, all done by people working under the stringent restrictions of timetables and deadlines. Yet their work is truly inventive, and makes a great contribution to Europe's contemporary art. It is the colloquial art of our time, seen by the man in the street in his — and her — millions. And, while such talent exists, there is no reason for anyone to be bombarded by unsatisfactory images.

In this respect alone, all companies — as well as many individuals — should be aware of the importance of well conceived and well executed artwork. We all have a responsibility towards each other to ensure that our environment remains free from visual pollution. For, while industrial pollution is horrific, visual pollution is inexcusable. Posters, newspapers, television, the cinema, books and magazines should be seen as galleries for the art of our time. In contrast to these living galleries, the national art collections of Europe have become dead areas — tombs for the genius of past artists. It is my belief that such work should be made more readily available to the public by being put into freely accessible living areas such as airports, railway stations, resorts, office blocks and other public buildings.

It may be argued that art from such a different time has no place outside the national collections. But much of any society's contemporary art has had a functional element. Portraits and war scenes, religious motifs and paintings of important events have had as much to say about the social condition of the day as does today's art commissioned for the mass media. And, in an age of mass communication, well executed art should play an important part in shaping the society we live in. Media art can offer a greater service to society than art that is shut away in museums. Thus there remains a real responsibility towards the public on the part of those who commission art. It is also the responsibility of the public to insist on good art.

The artists working for today's mass media deserve full recognition for their work, as much as it deserves to be seen by a wider public. They have a vital role to fulfil, and an important contribution to make to our lives.

List of all illustrators who have ever been in American Illustration

Mick Aarestrup
Jeffrey L. Adams
Mark H. Adams
Daniel Adel
Carlos A.L. Aguirre
Brian Ajhar
Maciek Albrecht
John Alcorn
Stephen Alcorn
Boris Allejo
Julian Allen
Terry Allen
Thomas B. Allen
Robert Clyde Anderson
Thomas Applegate
Marshall Arisman
Angela Arnet
Michael Aron
David Ayriss
Thomas Bachtell
Scott Baldwin
Roman Balicki
Jill Banashek
Istvan Banyai
Sergio Baradat
Cathy Barancik
Karen Barbour
Michelle Barnes
Deborah Barrett
Lynda Barry
Michael Bartalos
Caty Bartholomew
Kent H. Barton
Bascove
Gary Baseman
Earl C. Bateman III
Glen H. Batkin
Philippe Beha
Deborah A. Beldring
Catharine Bennett
Jamie Bennett
Mike Benny
Nina Berkson
Guy Billout
Paul Binkley
Maris Bishofs
Patricia Blackwell
Patrick Blackwell
Mary Lynn Blatsutta
Henry C. Blazer
R.O. Blechman
Cathie Bleck
Linda Bleck
Barry Blitt
Nancy Blowers
Christoph Blumrich

Alex Boies
Juan Botas
Richard J. Bouchard, Jr.
Joel Bower
Bill Boyko
Alaiyo Bradshaw
Braldt Bralds
Lee Lee Brazeal
Steve Brodner
Philip Brooker
Lou Brooks
Calef Brown
Roger Brown
Salvador Bru
Jim Buckels
Christine Bunn
Wendy Burden
Philip Burke
Trent Burleson
Charles Burns
David A. Burt
Llynne Buschman
Gerald Bustamante
Stephen Byram
Gianni Caccia
Kathy Calderwood
Kirk Caldwell
Dave Calver
John Camejo
Harry Cambpell
Kim Carlson
Larry W. Carroll
Patrick Lynn Carson
Steve Carver
Andrew Castrucci
Ron Chan
Denise Chapman
Bill Charmatz
Mark Chiarello
Darren Ching
Margaret Chodos-Irvine
Roger Chouinard
James C. Christensen
Sandra Christensen
Pete Christman
Tom Christopher
Seymour Chwast
Joseph Ciardiello
Greg Clarke
Jerry Clemens
Francesco Clemente
Judy Clifford
Lindee Climo
Alan E. Cober
Leslie Cober
Sue Coe
Santiago Cohen
John Collier
Raul Colon
Betzaida Concepcion
William Cone
Cheryl Cooper

Heather Cooper
Christopher Copeland
Copie
Ray-Mel Cornelius
Michael Corris
James Costello
Jerome Couelle
Normand Cousineau
Neverne K. Covington
David Cowles
Kinuko Y. Craft
Daniel Craig
John Craig
Denise Chapman Crawford
Robert Crawford
David Croland
Brian Cronin
Jose Cruz
Julia Cruz
David Lee Csicsko
Pat Cummings
Robert M. Cunningham
Tom Curry
Becky Cutler
Stephan Daigle
Howard Danelowitz
Dick Daniels
Bill Davis
Paul Davis
John Dawson
Rob Day
Peter de Seve
James Deacon
Greg Dearth
Merritt Dekle
Etienne Delessert
Oscar Demejo
Roger T. DeMuth
Catherine Denvir
Isabelle Dervaux
David Diaz
Tom Dillon
Harvey Dinnerstein
Sandra Dionisi
Jeff Dodson
Tom Dolphens
Michael Doret
Curt Doty
Blair Drawson
Debbie Drechsler
Henrik Drescher
Eric Drooker
Patricia Dryden
Andrzej Dudzinski
Joe Duffy
Fritz Dumville
Regan Dunnick
Nina Duran
Bernard Durin
Cameron Eagle
Sean Earley

Tony Eastman
Richard Egielski
Frederic Eibner
Jack Endewelt
James Endicott
Randall Enos
Wolf Erlbruch
Mike Esk
Julie Evans
Dolores Fairman
Perry Farrell and Casey
Teresa Fasoline
Robert Fassl
Ann Field
Judy Filippo
Jeanne Fisher
Mark S. Fisher
Tony Fitzpatrick
Joe Flaming
Joe Fleming
Vivienne Flesher
Jean Michel Folon
Walton Ford
Bob Fortier
Patric Fourshe
David Frampton
Douglas Fraser
Val Fraser
Craig Frazier
Lisa French
Gail Freund
Marvin Friedman
Dagmar Frinta
Maria Friske
Kristen Funkhouser
Tim Gabor
Victor Gadino
Nicholas Gaetano
Cynthia Gale
Chris Gall
David Gambale
Gene Garbowski
Frank Gargiulo
Allen Garns
Marie-Louise Gay
Warren Gebert
Gail Geltner
Audra Geras
Ben Gibson
Michael Gibson
Ralph Giguere
Chuck Gillies
Max Ginsburg
Robert Giusti
Guy Gladwell
Milton Glaser
Alex Gnidziejko
David Lance Goines
Jeff Gold
David Goldin
Bart Goldman

Robert Goldstrom
Carter Goodrich
Scott Gordley
Josh Gosfield
Dale Gottlieb
Carolyn Gowdy
Alexa Grace
Lynda Gray
Rodney Alan Greenblat
Gene Greif
Mel Griefinger
Alex Grey
Melissa Grimes
Robert Grossman
Steven Guarnaccia
Amy Guip
Walter Gurbo
John Hagen
Mick Haggerty
Bob Hambly
Michael Hampshire
Fran Hardy
Greg Harlin
Jennifer Harris
Martin Harris
Jessie Hartland
Margaret Hathaway
Ron Hauge
Karel Havlicek
Traci Haymans
Phillip Hays
Gary Head
Deborah Healy
Becky Heavner
Jim Heimann
Garnet Henderson
Hayes Henderson
Sandra Hendler
Patrick Henley
Cary Henrie
John Sherlock Hersey
Richard Hess
Buddy Hickerson
Lance Hidy
Sandra Higashi
Amy Hill
Fred Hilliard
Pamela Hobbs
Jamie Hogan
Wendy Hoile
Brad Holland
Gay W. Holland
Nigel Holmes
Katheryn Holt
John Hom
Amy Horowitz
John H. Howard
Anne Howeson
Margaret Huber
Phil Huling
Cathy Hull

Scott W. Hunt
Thomas Hunt
Roger Huyssen
John Hyatt
Mirko Ilic
Yoshohiro Inomoto
Seth Jaben
Jeff Jackson
Kathryn Jacobi
Rick Jacobson
Nancy Jakubowski
Bill James
Christopher Jarrin
Frances Jetter
John Jinks
David A. Johnson
Doug Johnson
Joel Peter Johnson
Lonni Sue Johnson
Shelly E. Johnson
Steve Johnson
V. Courtlandt Johnson
Russell O. Jones
Sabrina Jones
R.E. Jordan
Ken Joudrey
Jeff Jurich
Maira Kalman
Laura Karp
Ellen Kaska
Alex Katz
Earl Keleny
Gary Kelly
Lauren Keswick
Tim C. Kilian
J.D. King
Julia King
Tracy Kirshenbaum
John Kleber
Michael S. Klein
Renee Klein
Jane Kleinman
Nancy Klobucar
Michael Klotz
Barbara Klunder
Jean-Christian Knaff
Peter Knock
George F. Kocar
Jerzy Kolacz
Robert Kopecky
Edward Koren
Ira M. Korman
Bill Kovacs
Stephen Kroninger
Mark Kseniak
Kuniyasu
Anita Kunz
Peter Kuper
Joan Kurtz
Kevin Kurtz
Lili Lakich

Mark G. Langeneckert
Philippe Lardy
Pamela Lee
Pierre Le-Tan
Bryan Leister
David Lesh
Marie Lessard
Birney Lettick
Laura Levine
David Levine
Tim Lewis
Martine Lieberman
Malcolm T. Liepke
Skip Liepke
Ron Lightburn
David Limrite
Nicky Lindeman
Ed Lindlof
Warren Linn
Kandy Jean Littrell
Sue Llewellyn
Lindsey Loch
David Loew
John C. Long
Robert Longo
Janet Longstreth
Rafael Lopez
Jeannette Louie
Rick Lovell
Victoria Lowe
Jessica Knight Loy
Ruth Lozner
Abbe Lubell
Dennis Luzak
Kevin Lyles
Matthew Lynaugh
Fred Lynch
Chris Lyons
Steve Lyons
Michael Mabry
Ross MacDonald
Daniel Maffia
Katherine Mahoney
Matt Mahurin
Kam Mak
Richard Mantel
Mark Marek
Ruth Marten
John Martin
John Martinez
Ken Maryanski
George Masi
Robert Mason
Petra Mathers
Robin Matsuyoshi
Marvin Mattelson
John Mattos
Kevin P. McCloskey
Stan McCray
Mercedes McDonald

Jerry McDonald
Patrick McDonnell
Michael McGar
Michael McGurl
Wilson McLean
Gregory McMickin
James McMullan
Richard McNeel
Robert Meganck
Elwyn Mehlman
Thessy Mehrain
Paul Meisel
Gary Mele
Scott Menchin
Andy Meyer
Gary Meyer
Sara Midda
Eugene Mihaesco
Daryl R. Miles
Wendell Minor
Kenny Mirman
Carel Moiseiwitsch
Clement Mok
Jack Molloy
Ken Monda
Desmond Montague
David Montiel
Gary Mooney
Leonard E. Morgan
Jerry Moriarty
Hideaki Morita
Alison Moritsugu
Jennifer Morla
Frank K. Morris
Hilary Mosberg
Geoffrey Moss
Donna Muir
Paula Munck
San Murata
Alex Murawski
Joel Nakamura
Bill Nelson
Meredith Nemirov
Barbara Nessim
Robert Neubecker
Ann Neumann
Jeffrey Newbury
Simon Ng
Craig Nielsen
Adam Niklewicz
Tomio Nitto
Dennis Noble
Wil Northener
Istvan Nyari
Mel Odom
Masaaki Ogai
J. Rafal Olbinski
Frank Olinsky
Mark Oliver
Jose Ortega
Anthony Pack
John Jude Palencar

Gary Panter
Yves Paquin
Michael Paraskevas
Richard Parent
Susan Parente
Robert Andrew Parker
John Parks
Melanie Marder Parks
Pamela Higgins Patrick
Rick Patrick
Celeste Paulick
C.F. Payne
Beth Peck
Everett Peck
Judy Pedersen
Daniel Pelavin
Robert Peluce
Mark Penberthy
Donna Perrone
Rex Peteet
Bob Peters
Bryan L. Peterson
Philippe Petit-Roulet
Max Phillips
Archil Pichkhadze
Morgan Pickard
Steve Pietzsch
Paola Piglia
Patrick Pigott
Ted Pitts
Dave Plunkert
Jean Francois Podevin
Lissa Pollie
Ian Pollock
Bradley O. Pomeroy
Alexandru Preiss
Glenn Priestley
Camille Przewodek
Don Ivan Punchatz
Liz Pyle
Mike Quon
Greg Ragland
Ralle
Dan Reed
Doug Renfro
John Resi
Joel Resnicoff
Scott Reynolds
David Ricceri
Dave Ridley
Lana Rigsby
Robert Risko
Larry Rivers
Randy Roberts
Robert Rodriguez
Lilla Rogers
Nevle Rogers
Paul Rogers
Javier Romero
Barry Root
Delro Rosco

Phil Rose
Jonathon Rosen
Marc Rosenthal
Laurie Rosenwald
Richard Ross
Sheba Ross
John Rush
Bill Russell
Anthony Russo
David Brendan Ryan
Kouichi Sakumoto
Joseph Salina
Barbara Samuels
David Sandlin
Cindy Sandro
Richard Schlecht
Ward Schumaker
Michael Schwab
Gary Schwartz
Joanie Schwartz
Sara Schwartz
Cathryn Schwing
Tom Sciacca
Julie Scott
J. Otto Seibold
Alison Seiffer
Henry Selick
Michael Sell
Joseph Sellars
Marsha Serafin
Thom Sevalrud
David Shannon
Tim Sheaffer
Maurice Sherman
Neil Shigley
Steve Shock
Don Sibley
Lee & Mary Sievers
Martin Sigmund
Valerie Sinclair
Walter Sipser
Peter Sis
Collete Slade
William A. Sloan
Aaron Smith
Doug Smith
Ed Smith
Elwood H. Smith
Jeffrey J. Smith
Lane Smith
Laura Smith
Leo Smith
Monica Smith
Owen Smith
Edgar Soberon
Edward Sorel
Ed Soyka
Greg Spalenka
Paul Sparagano
Art Spiegelman
Pete Spino

Chris Spollen
Barton E. Stabler
Nancy Stahl
James Staunton
Ralph Steadman
James Steinberg
Dugald Stermer
Amahlia Stevens
Randy Stevens
Dave Stevenson
Marcia Stieger
Barron Storey
Gwyn M. Stramler
Mark Strathy
David Street
Don Sullivan
Jozef Sumichrast
David Suter
Sara Swan
Leslie Szabo
Thomas Szumowski
Nick Taggart
David Tamura
Marla Tarbox
Malcolm Tarlofsky
Ramon Gonzalez Teja
Peter Tengler
James E. Tennison
Michael Thibodeau
Troy Thomas
James Thorpe
Bonnie Timmons
Kathy Todd
Cathleen Toelke
Tip Toland
Sam Tomasello
Cristobal Toral
Brenda Lee Tracy
Michael Trossman
Ezra N. Tucker
James Tughan
Pol Turgeon
Paul D. Turnbaugh
Ray Turner
Robert Tuska
Jean Tuttle
Mark Ulriksen
Jack Unruh
Peter Vahlefeld
Michel Guire Vaka
Anton Van Dalen
John Van Fleet
John Van Hamersveld
Ken Vares
Kurt Vargo
Maurice Vellekoop
Roxana Villa
Gary Viskupic
Stefano Vitale
Frank Viva
Bill Vuksanovich

Robert Wade
Friedrich Karl Waechter
James Wahlberg
Carol Wald
David Art Wales
Christine Walker
Tracy Walker
David Wallin
Susan Walp
Andy Warhol
Michele Warner
Karen Watson
Stan Watts
Mark Weakley
Robert Weaver
Thomas Webb
Scott Webber
Nick Weingarten
Philippe Weisbecker
Amie Weitzman
Anders Wenngren
Michael Whelan
Charles White III
Debra White
Terry Widener
Roy Wiemann
Mick Wiggins
David Wilcox
Kent Williams
Linden Wilson
Rob Wilson
Nicholas Wilton
Chuck Wimmer
Robert Wisnewski
Deborah Withey-Culp
Michael Witte
David Wojnarowicz
Paul Wolf
Bruce Wolfe
Efram Wolff
Wojchech Wolynski
Martin Wong
Rob Wood
Thomas Woodruff
Janet Wooley
Scott Wright
Janet Yake
Paul Yalowitz
Mary Yanish
Etty Yaniv
Robert Yarber
Lisa Young
M. Christopher Zacharow
Daniel Zakrozemski
Gary Zamchick
Rene Zamic
Brian Zick
Dennis Ziemienski
Bob Zuba
Fanny Zucchiatti
Darryl Zudeck

ILLUSTRATORS

A

Mick Aarestrup 30
364 Atlantic Avenue
Brooklyn, NY 11217

Maciek Albrecht 74, 75
PO Box 30115
New York, NY 10011

B

Istvan Banyai 142
13220 Valleyheart Drive
Studio City, CA 91604

Sergio Baradat 163
210 West 70th Street
New York, NY 10023

Karen Barbour 147, 154
3444 21st Street
San Francisco, CA 94110

Gary Baseman 39-41, 148
443 12th Street
Brooklyn, NY 11215

Deborah A. Beldring 96
7108 Hollis Street N.E.
Albuquerque, NM 87109

Barry Blitt 165
58 West 87th Street
New York, NY 10024

Calef Brown 112
3603 Faris Drive
Los Angeles, CA 90034

Philip Burke 26-29
163 College Street
Buffalo, NY 14201

Gerald Bustamante 114
4528 North 44th Street
San Diego, CA 92115

C

Dave Calver 149
70 Stoneham Drive
Rochester, NY 14625

Harry Campbell 132
Washington Street
Jersey City, NJ 07302

Tom Christopher 158
11-51 30th Road
Long Island City, NY 11102

Seymour Chwast 62
The Pushpin Group
215 Park Avenue South
New York, NY 10003

Greg Clarke 155
844 9th Street
Santa Monica, CA 90403

Sue Coe 60
214 East 84th Street
New York, NY 10028

Betzaida Concepcion 176
c/o Bullet Space
292 East 3rd Street
New York, NY 10009

David Cowles 121
Box 87
Gorham, NY 14461

Daniel Craig 143
118 East 26th Street
Minneapolis, MN 55404

Brian Cronin 54-57, 119
8 Terenure Park
Terenure, Dublin,
6W Ireland

Tom Curry 76
Prickly Pear Studio
1101 Cap. of Texas Hwy. So.
Austin, TX 78746

D

Greg Dearth 104
4041 Beal Road
Franklin, OH 45005

Blair Drawson 20
355 Mathers Avenue
West Vancouver, BCanada V7S 1H2

Henrik Drescher 38
PO Box 59
Durham, NY 12422

Eric Drooker 175
PO Box 1351
New York, NY 10009

Patty Dryden 124
575 West End Avenue
New York, NY 10024

E

Jack Endewelt 151
50 Riverside Drive
New York, NY 10024

F

Perry Farrell and Casey 120
c/o Warner Brothers Records
3300 Warner Blvd.
Burbank, CA 91505

Ann Field 106, 107
2910 16th Street
Santa Monica, CA 90405

Tony FitzPatrick 22
525 S. Dearborn Street
Chicago, IL 60605

Joe Fleming 59
487 Mortimer Avenue
Toronto, ONT
Canada M4J 2G6

Douglas Fraser 65
340 Sharon Avenue S.W.
Calgary, ALB
Canada T3C 2G7

Maria Friske 122, 123
684-C Park Avenue
Rochester, NY 14607-3022

G

David Goldin 156
111 4th Avenue
New York, NY 10003

Josh Gosfield 72, 84, 115, 118
682 Broadway
New York, NY 10012

Steven Guarnaccia 47-49
430 West 14th Street
New York, NY 10014

Amy Guip 61, 133-137
430 Lafayette Street
New York, NY 10003

H

Jessie Hartland 105
165 William Street
New York, NY 10038

Brad Holland 33-35, 127-129
96 Greene Street
New York, NY 10012

J

Nancy Jakubowski 150
252 Doyle Avenue
Providence, RI 02906

Sabrina Jones 178
215 East 4th Street
New York, NY 10009

K

John Kleber 31
314 Fifth Avenue South
Minneapolis, MN 55415

Michael Klotz 131
235 East 27th Street
New York, NY 10016

Anita Kunz 52
230 Ontario Street
Toronto, ONT
Canada M5A 2V5

Peter Kuper 70, 71, 95
250 West 99th Street
New York, NY 10025

L

Philippe Lardy 19, 98
478 West Broadway
New York, NY 10012

Laura Levine 130
444 Broome Street
New York, NY 10013

M

Ross MacDonald 21
27-1/2 Morton Street
New York, NY 10014

Mark Marek 170
42 Erie Street
Dumont, NJ 07628

Ruth Marten 167
81 Irving Place
New York, NY 10003

James McMullan 113
222 Park Avenue South
New York, NY 10003

Scott Menchin 32
640 Broadway
New York, NY 10012

Andy Meyer 159
465 West 23rd Street
New York, NY 10011

Sara Midda 86-93
708 Broadway
New York, NY 10003

Paula Munck 125
150 Farnham Avenue
Toronto, ONT
Canada M4V 1H5

N

Craig Nielsen 97
Box 45
Reserve, MT 59258

O

Jose Ortega 63, 99, 160
524 East 82nd Street
New York, NY 10028

P

Philippe Petit-Roulet 101
63 Rue De La Grange-Aux-Belles
75010 Paris, France

Archil Pichkhadze 162
161 Roebling Street
Brooklyn, NY 11211

R

David Ricceri 51
505 Court Street
Brooklyn, NY 11231

Jonathon Rosen 80-83
408 2nd Street
Brooklyn, NY 11215

Laurie Rosenwald 64
11 West 30th Street
New York, NY 10001

S

Kouichi Sakumoto 161
9 Barrow Street
New York, NY 10014

David Sandlin 100
58 East 1st Street
New York, NY 10003

Cindy Sandro 152
92 26th Street N.E.
Atlanta, GA 30309

Joanie Schwartz 77
300 Grand Street
Hoboken, NJ 07030

J. Otto Seibold 42-45
41 East 22nd Street
New York, NY 10010

Henry Selick 171
222 Ashton Avenue
San Francisco, CA 94112

David Shannon 94
306 East 50th Street
New York, NY 10022

Walter Sipser 174
166 Suffolk Street
New York, NY 10002

Lane Smith 67-69, 85, 141
43 West 16th Street
New York, NY 10011

Amahlia Stevens 73
1938 Del Mar
Laguna Beach, CA 92651

Don Sullivan 166
912 South Telluride Street
Aurora, CO 80017

T

Malcolm Tarlofsky 53
5420 Manila Avenue
Oakland, CA 94618

Pol Turgeon 111
5187 Jeanne-Mance #3
Montreal, QUE
Canada H2V 4K2

U

Mark Ulriksen 153
680 8th Street
San Francisco, CA 94103

Jack Unruh 66
2706 Fairmount
Dallas, TX 75201

V

Peter Vahlefeld 164
315 Central Park West
New York, NY 10025

Anton Van Dalen 179
166 Avenue A
New York, NY 10009

Frank Viva 46
12 Birch Avenue
Toronto, ONT
Canada M4V 1C8

Stefano Vitale 36, 37
478 Bergen Street
Brooklyn, NY 11217

W

Thomas Webb 157
218 Degraw Street
Brooklyn, NY 11231

Philippe Weisbecker 50, 126
136 Waverly Place
New York, NY 10014

Mick Wiggins 58
1103 Amador Avenue
Berkeley, CA 94707

David Wojnarowicz 177
c/o Bullet Space
292 East 3rd Street
New York, NY 10009

Janet Woolley 23-25
c/o Alan Lynch
155 Sixth Avenue
New York, NY 10013

ART DIRECTORS

Altomore, Lisa 61
Armario, David 147
Bartholomay, Lucy 32
Berry, Pamela 36, 37
Bleiweiss, Richard 33
Burtis, Neville 73
Bustamante, Gerald 114
Campbell, Harry 132
Carson, David 69
Christensen, Sara 31, 39-41
Cowles, David 121-123
Cuyler, Jolene 23, 29
Davis, Paul 50, 63, 72, 126
Davis, Ron 171
Drummond, Stacy 112
Dunjko, Carmen 20, 21
Farr, Amy 133-137
Friedlander, Ira 77
Garlan, Judy 42-45
Garner, Anne 96, 97
Hanson, Paul 86-93
Haroutuin, Georges 59
Harris, Nancy 65
Hein, Kevin 30
Hoffman, Joanne 58
Hoffman, Steven 52, 53
Johanknecht, Steven 105
Kent, Nancy V. 46
Kuper, Peter 71
Leach, Molly 85
LeWerke, Ria 124
McCutcheon, Neill 51
Morris, Don 48, 49
Newman, Susan 94
Nissen, Melanie 115
Palecek, Jane 38
Phillips, Jennifer 127-129
Pickel, David 47
Piercy, Clive 106, 107
Porter, J. 76
Pospischil, Hans-Georg 35, 62
Rambaldi, George 55
Renfro, Doug 25
Riccardi, Douglas 64
Rice, Nancy 74, 75
Russek, Jim 113
Segal, Jackie 19
Selbert, Clifford 143
Selick, Henry 171
Simmons-Lynch, Julie 70
Smith, Nancy 24
Staebler, Tom 22
Steele, Tommy 130
Stout, D.J. 34
Suares, J.C. 142

Takahashi, Drew 170
Tremain, Kerry 28
Watson, Cheryl 125
Wilson, Fo 54
Wong, Tracy 104
Woodward, Fred 56, 57, 66-68, 141, 167

DESIGN DIRECTORS

Caldwell, Cathy 61
Grossman, Michael 26, 27, 60

DESIGNERS

Anderson, Gail 56, 57
Andrews, Jill 51
Belcher, Julie 31, 39-41
Burns, Andrea 25
Cronin, Brian 119
Dickie, Jill 21
Fernandez, Teresa 52, 53
Fey, Jeffrey 130
Figurski, John 70
Fournel, Jocelyne 111
Gibbs, Scott 20
Gilmore-Barnes, Robin 42-45
Gosfield, Josh 118
Klotz, Michael 131
Kondo, Linda 143
Korjenek, Kristen 22
Kula, Anna 60
Lee, Sheri G. 98-101
Lingen, Rez 80-83
Marek, Mark 170
McMillen, Nancy 34
Michaelson, Mark 27
Newman, Robert 26
Ochs, Marianna 126
Recchion, Tom 120
Rosenwald, Laurie 64
Sessa, Marsha 28
Shafer, Mark 29
Zaitschek, Risa 50

DESIGN GROUPS

Barton-Giller 127-129
Capitol Records Art Dept. 130
Clifford Selbert Design 143
Paul Davis Studio 126
Spade & Archer 142

WRITERS

Abeel, Erica 61
Benatar, Giselle 26
Boresage, Robert L. 56, 57
Boucher, Norman 32
Brownell, Kelly, PhD. 77
Bryce, Robert 34
Burr, Ty 60
Clarke, Lee 42-45
Davidouici, Sorin 74
Davis, Lisa 38
Emerson, Steven A. 33
Evens, Paul 67
Fallows, James 68
Fissinger, Laura 39-41
Fitzpatrick, Tony 22
Frick, David 66
Green, Stanley 19
Hale, Judson D. 76
Hazleton, Lesley 65
Heinrich-Jose, Von Ingrid 35
Hitt, Jack 25
Hofler, Bob 23, 29
Houseman, Doug 58
Kaplan, Jim 52, 53
Kennedy, Dana 47
Lerner, Preston 73
Mogg, Tad 75
Newton, Nathan 69
O'Connell, Anna 58
Rossi, Vicky 125
Roustis, Georgia 51
Schecter, Cathy 31
Schwartz, Von Christopher 62
Shuchman, Miriam 46
Spake, Amanda 36, 37
Talbot, Stephen 28
Wilkes, Michael 46
Williams, Clay 104
Wulf, Steve 52, 53

AUTHORS

Castrucci, Andrew 174
Coen, Nadia 174
Ionesco, Eugene 94
Joyce, James 97
Matheson, Richard 84
Melville, Herman 96
Midda, Sara 86-93
Morales, Frank 174
Rosen, Jonathon 80-83
Sinclair, Upton 95
Smith, Lane 85
Vargas Llosa, Marie 147

EDITORS

Castrucci, Andrew 174
Castrucci, Paul 174
Coen, Nadia 174
Conner, Jeff 84
Garner, Anne 96, 97
Hayes, Regina 85
Kovalchick, Sally 86-93
Lardy, Philippe 98-101
Ortega, Jose 98-101
Roberts, Wade 95
Ruckenstein, Lelia 94

ADVERTISING AGENCIES

BNY Advertising 105
Goodby, Berlin & Silverstein 104
P.H.D. 106, 107
Russek Advertising 113

CLIENTS

All Quebec Exhibition 111
Barney's America 105
Bicycling West, Inc. 114
Clark's of England 104
Columbia Records 112
Dayton Hudson Department Stores 125
Elektra Records 170
Jazz Furniture Gallery 106, 107
Lincoln Center Theatre 113
MTV Networks 171
New School for Social Research 127-129
New York Botanical Garden 143
Nexus World-Japan 126
Polygram Records 131
RCA Records 124
Sony Music 112
Virgin Records 115

ANIMATORS

Goldsmith, Chris 170
Klatte, Owen 171
Leighton, Eric 171
Thomas, Trey 171

PRODUCTION COMPANIES

Selick Projects 171

PRODUCERS

Adams, Phyllis 170
Payson, John 171

DIRECTORS

Przyluska, Lidia 170
Selick, Henry 171

MUSIC COMPOSITION

Flansburgh, John 170
Linnell, John 170
The Residents 171

PUBLICATIONS

American Health Magazine 77
The Atlantic Monthly 42-45
Beach Culture 69
The Boston Globe Magazine 32
Byte Magazine 74, 75
Egg Magazine 64
Entertainment Weekly 26, 27, 60
Esquire 147
Footwear News 104
Frankfurter Allgemeine Magazin 35, 62
Good Health Magazine 46
Havoc 30
Heavy Metal 70
Homemakers Magazine 59
In Health Magazine 38
LA Style 73
Longevity Magazine 54
Lui Magazine 55
Mac World 58
Metropolitan Home 48, 49
Mother Jones Magazine 28
Ms. Magazine 24
Musician Magazine 133-137
New Woman Magazine 61
The New York Times Magazine 65
Newsday Magazine 19
Penthouse Magazine 33
Playboy Magazine 22
The Plain Dealer Magazine 47
Rolling Stone 56, 57, 66, 67, 68, 141
Sassy Magazine 51
Saturday Night Magazine 20, 21
Savvy Woman 36, 37
Special Report 25
Special Report/Family 39-41
Special Report/Health 31
Sports Illustrated 52, 53
Texas Monthly 34
US Magazine 23, 29
Wigwag 50, 63, 72
Yankee Magazine 76

PUBLISHING COMPANIES

Affiliated Publications, Inc. 32
American Express Publishing 73
An Post 119
The Atlantic Monthly Corporation 42-45
Berkley Books 95
Better Living Inc. 69
The Bozarts Press 96, 97
Bullet 174
Family Media 36, 37
Forbes 64
Foundation for National Progress 28
Frankfurter All. Zeitung 35, 62
General Media 54
Gin & Comix 98-101
Gousha/Simon & Schuster 142
Hippocrates, Inc. 38
HM Communications 70
INX/United Features 71
Lang Communications 24
MacWorld Communications 58
McGraw-Hill 74, 75
Meredith Corporation 48, 49
Murdoch Magazines 61
The New York Times 46, 65
Paragon House 94
Penthouse 33
The Plain Dealer Publishing Company 47
Playboy Enterprises 22
Poote Press 80-83
Purgatory Pie Press 118
Rayocine Studios 30
Readers Digest Magazines 77
Sassy Publishers, Inc. 51
Saturday Night Magazine Inc. 20, 21
Scream Press 84
Straight Arrow Publishers 23, 29, 56, 57, 66-68, 141
Telemedia 59
Texas Monthly Magazine 34
Time-Warner Inc. 26, 27, 52, 53, 60
Times-Mirror 19
Viking Penguin 85
Warner Brothers Records 120
Whittle Communications 25, 31, 39-41
Wigwag Magazine Company 50, 63, 72
Workman Publishing Company 86-93
Yankee Publishing, Inc. 76